They suffer in faith...

Stories of the life transforming
work of God among and
through the people of Haiti

By April Perry

All proceeds from the sales of this book will go directly to help the work in Haiti through Luke's Mission, Inc. Luke's Mission is a Christian non profit organization that works in Haiti supporting education for health care providers and advancing public health projects both in urban and rural settings.

Contributions are tax deductible and can be sent to:

Luke's Mission, Inc
1403 Mason Road
Durham, NC 27712

At the time of publishing the climate in Haiti remains turbulent and dangerous. For security purposes, the names in this book have been changed. Christians are in danger of abduction and harm from gangs and rebel insurgents for simply claiming Christ through their work in the church. Kidnappings have increased among those with American friends. The abductors perceive Americans as having unlimited financial resources making these Christians greater targets for ransom. It would be my desire to feel free to name these saints of God but, in order that their work can go on, I have altered all the names in these pages except for my own. I pray for the day they may be named openly and freely.

Dedication

*This book is dedicated by my dearest Haitian friend, Remy,
whose name I wish very much I could put in these pages but whose
name I don't for fear of a compromise to his and his family's safety.
Remy has been an inspiration to me in my Christian walk like no
one else in my life. His sweet spirit, sensitive heart, spirit of love
and compassion for his people are examples for us all. His desire
to overcome his situation to realize his dream and the work that
has had to go into that inspire me daily. My faith, which results
from nearly thirty years of walking with the Lord,
pales in comparison to his.*

*His friendship is a blessed gift to me.
It is to him that the words in this book are lovingly dedicated.*

Blest Are They[1]

Blest are they, the poor in spirit, theirs is the kingdom of God.
Blest are they, full of sorrow, they shall be consoled.

Rejoice! and be glad! Blessed are you, holy are you.
Rejoice! And be glad! Yours is the kingdom of God!

Blest are they, the lowly ones, they shall inherit the earth.
Blest are they who hunger and thirst, they shall have their fill.

Blest are they who show mercy, Mercy shall be theirs.
Blest are they, the pure of heart; they shall see God.

Blest are they who seek peace; they are the children of God.
Blest are they who suffer in faith: The glory of God is theirs.

Blest are you who suffer hate, all because of me.
Rejoice and be glad, yours is the kingdom:
Shine for all to see.

Rejoice! And be glad! Blessed are you, holy are you.
Rejoice! And be glad! Yours is the kingdom of God

Table of contents:

Dedication v

Acknowledgements xiii

Forward xv

Map of Haiti..xvii

Chapter One
    Hope in the Darkness 21

Chapter Two
    A Matter of perspective...27

Chapter Three
    My Name is Remy 33

Chapter Four
    A Lesson Before Dying...39

Chapter Five
    To Suffer With Others 45

Chapter Six
    The Gift 53

Chapter Seven
    Position Yourself to Receive a Blessing 61

Chapter Eight
    "If Just a Cup of Water…" 65

Chapter Nine
    Little is Much in Balais, Haiti 75

Chapter Ten
    But God, *Every* Need 85

Chapter Eleven
    Lord, Teach Me to Pray 91

Chapter Twelve
    The Hem of His Garment 97

Chapter Thirteen
    Voodoo-A Wolf in Sheep's Clothing 105

Chapter Fourteen
    The Road to Garema 111

Chapter Fifteen
    Refiners Fire...121

Chapter Sixteen
    God is Not Surprised...129

Chapter Seventeen
    The Situation here…It is Terrible 137

Chapter Eighteen
Ransomed 143

Chapter Nineteen
The Funeral 153

Chapter Twenty
A Heavy Yet Blessed Burden 157

Chapter Twenty One
The Lone Starfish 161

Chapter Twenty Two
My Life-A Designated Donation 169

Chapter Twenty Three
The New City of the Son 181

Chapter Twenty Four
Haiti, August, 2005 185

References 189

Appendix
Luke's Mission, Inc. 191
Haiti-General Statistics 194
Haiti-Comparative Statistics 197

Acknowledgements:

I am grateful to many people for their assistance and support in the compilation of these stories. Many thanks to Shelia who accompanied me on my first trip and now stands next to me as we work together for the long term in Haiti. Her love for the Haitians and me has been a sustaining force.

Thanks to my parents, family and many friends including Ron, Shelly, Gayle, Don, Sabrina, Gordon, Jackie, Brian and the many folk at Blacknall Memorial Presbyterian Church and Ridgecrest Baptist Seniors class who have surrounded me with support during good and difficult times of work. I have been touched many times as they have seen needs in Haiti and stepped up to fill them.

Thanks to my mom, Joyce Perry, for her assistance in editing this book.

A special thanks to Ben Lichius who, though unable to travel to Haiti, has given much in service to the people of Haiti and our work there through his artistry and talents. His cover design of this book was a blessing that I cannot adequately find words to express.

Thanks to Wally Turnbull for his lifetime of service to Christ and the Haitian people and for the use of his photograph for the cover.

To Katherine, Quinn, Taylor, Sarah, Lydia, Zeke and Judah: Thank you for praying for the children of Haiti. Jesus hears your prayers each night and watches over them just as He watches over you.

To Gina and Beth: I couldn't do my work in Haiti without your help. Thank you.

Finally I want to thank all of the people in Haiti who have impacted my life in a most significant way-all whose names are disguised here-they are the stars in this book-Jean, Pastor Auguste, Remy, Pastor Charles, Sr. Constance, Sr. Cecilia...you are the ones who are truly blest because you suffer in faith. M' priye Bondye bay ou anpil fos pou chak jou. (May God strengthen you each moment of every day.)

May God convict us all of our corporate sins for not caring for the poor as we should and lead us to salvation through repentance and service.

Forward

Haiti came into my life in May, 2001 when I joined a medical mission trip that my local church was sponsoring to a poor slum in Haiti. Never in a million years would I have realized the journey that those 10 days would begin for me. It has clearly been one of complete transformation in my walk with Christ.

I have come to see the critical nature that service to each other is in understanding and developing the character of Christ, both in my life and the lives of others. I have come to realize that, like silver in it's refining, it is in suffering that we are purified; that our faith cannot grow unless it is tested and for that reason we should count it all joy when we receive trials (James 1:2).

God is transforming my life though His work in Haiti. For that I am truly grateful to the Haitian people in a way that would be hard to express in words.

Blest are the Haitians, who suffer in faith, for the glory of God is theirs. My prayer is that you will see that on the pages which follow.

HAITI

75 km

North Atlantic Ocean

Île de la Tortuga

Port-de-Paix

Cap-Haïtien

Gonaïves

Golfe de la Gonâve

St.-Marc

Ti Rivyè

Hispaniola

Île de la Gonâve

Jérémie

PORT-AU-PRINCE

Jacmel

Les Cayes

Caribbean Sea

"Blest are they that suffer in faith
For the glory of God is theirs"
-Matthew 5:10-
(Paraphrased) [1]

"Has not God chosen
those who are poor in the eyes of the world
to be rich in faith
and to inherit the kingdom
He promised those who love him?"
James 2:5 (NIV)

CHAPTER ONE

Hope in the Darkness

"Wednesday, May 2, 2001

It is hard to find beauty here. Our team leader assures us there is some and it will have to be in the people. It doesn't appear to be anywhere else. Even my discriminating eye can find no wonders of God's creation here as I look out on this desolate place.

It's pretty amazing how quickly I have gone into the western version of a survival mode. My appearance, once somewhat important, has little consequence now. My main goal is to salvage as little comfort and relief from the heat as I can—it matters little what I look like in the process. Mascara, matching clothing, well coifed hair means nothing. And what I am feeling is only a fraction of what the Haitians must feel. A pink head band and a brown dress- who cares as long as it keeps the sweat out of my eyes.

I saw between 40 and 50 patients today. It was about mid day before I saw one who smiled and it so impressed me that I took her picture. The people here look so tired (many are anemic, some sickle cell), weary, and frequently in pain somewhere or the other.

Remy, my translator, was a real gift. He was quite capable and a true joy to be around. The work was physically (because of the heat,) mentally and emotionally exhausting. I was very tired at the end of the day.

God has not forsaken these people—I know that now, but He has asked them to bear a heavy burden for Him. Many people had problems our medicine could help for a time anyway. My most heart breaking moment today was telling a mother her 15 year old's problems were all rooted in his lack of food. I asked the translator, Remy, to ask her if she had money to buy more food—the only thing he would not translate the whole day. I was wearing my ignorance. Of course she had no money for food. If she did, she would have bought it.

We gave him some analgesics, iron and vitamins, but that was all I could offer, except the love of Christ, our Savior. And I did my best to offer that. As I took Maggie's suggestion to pray with every patient I saw, I was blessed. It was wearying but everyone said Oui, Oui."

~~~~~~~~~~~~~~~~~~~~~~~~~~~~~

That is the journal entry for one of my first days in Haiti. As you can see, my outlook on the situation was pretty bleak. Our work takes us to an urban slum of Port au Prince, the capital city of Haiti. In it, there are 500,000 people living without electricity, any form of sanitation, access to clean water or health care. All of this within the confines of 4 square miles. Unfortunately this area has the distinction of being the poorest slum in the western hemisphere.

The road to the clinic had pot holes as big as our truck. It is not unusual to see several children bathing in these pot holes following a rain storm. It is obvious why skin diseases are one of the most prevalent things we treated. We dispense soap from the pharmacy because it is like a drug there.

Raw sewage runs in the street-thus the requirement by our team leader to not wear open shoes to the clinic. And to wash you hands after tying your shoes. How often do we do that in the United States?

Our clinic is only one of two to serve nearly half a million people. Some people travel for days to arrive to see the "missionary doctors". It doesn't matter what level of health care provider one was, everyone was a "doktor blan".

Situated less than 500 miles from the United States borders, who would believe this degree of poverty and need would exist so close to our own borders. Built on a land fill, houses in this area-

and I use the term as loosely as one can- are made of used corrugated tin held up by sticks in each corner. Human waste is often disposed of by throwing it on the roofs. This slum has the distinction of being know as the poorest slum in the western hemisphere. Our outpatient clinic is only one of two available for the health care needs of the people of area.

However, even from the start I could see that the resources which were the most valuable to this small country, a country only about the size of our state of Maryland, are her human resources. If Haiti was to survive, it would be her people who would make that happen. And they have the resources to do just that but they won't be able to do it alone.

In the center of this vast land fill which serves as a home to nearly a half a million people, is an oasis known as the Christ's Church of the City. It is a complex surrounded by a 12 foot cement block wall with the typical Haitian security system-broken glass and/or razor wire embedded into concrete on the top blocks to prevent scaling of the wall. The gates were open frequently in our early work there.

Enclosed in this fortress like structure is a source of hope, the only one that many had in their entire lives. Behind the turquoise painted wall was a church which seated 3500 and most Sundays, until the last few months, was nearly full for at least one of the two services it held. There is also a school for 400 children ranging in ages from preschool to sixth grade. Our clinic building is the third building housed in this complex.

A simple concrete structure which had been upgraded over the years with sinks for running water, storage cabinets and shelving for the drugs located in the pharmacy as well as window air conditioners in two of the rooms, this building is the only access to medical care that many of the people in this slum had. In addition, when word reached the edges of the city and even the countryside that the American "doktor yo" ("doctors" in Haitian Kreyol) were coming, many people walk for hours to get there.

Our clinics are typically a week long. Usually on Sunday afternoon after church, before we do our regular clinics, we run a special clinic for the church leaders. These men and women don't get much recognition for their work in the church so it is a little perk that they can come to the clinic first. Because most of them are healthy or don't have serious health problems, it gives the team a chance to perfect their roles and for us to work out any bugs in our system prior to beginning a full week of clinics with the average Haitian patients we see, most of whom are pretty ill.

But the highlight of the week always was the two hour worship service which we would participate in on Sunday morning. Most of us couldn't speak Haitian Kreyol, one of two official languages in Haiti. French is the other and used nearly exclusively in schools, and places of business. However, Haitian Kreyol is the language of the people and the indigenous language of Haiti. Unfortunately it has come to be known as the language of the peasants, diminishing it of its beauty, simplicity, and removing it as a source of pride for most Haitians.

Regardless of the language in which people spoke or sang in the worship service at Christ's Church of the City, communication wasn't a problem because the language of the Spirit transcends all others. We sing with the Haitians, and their prayer time is one of the most powerful worship experiences I have experienced in my lifetime.

The stories which follow in this book will begin to show the transforming work of God in my own life through my work in Haiti. But that is only the beginning of the story. The transformation continues.

I have traveled to Haiti many times leading medical teams and traveling alone for work with a small village in a rural plain for Luke's Mission. I have come to see how repentance and service is the vehicle which God uses to begin to grow the character of Christ in my life. I have come to see how Jesus must have felt in many circumstances and why His teaching regarding the care of the poor and less fortunate took up so much of His teaching during His short three year ministry period.

Now, five years later, my outlook is not bleak at all. It is with gratitude that I thank our Heavenly Father for the great privilege of working side by side with His precious children in Haiti.

This is a love story—a story of my love for the Haitian people, their love for me and the love of a God that will not let me go. You will see in the stories that follow how those loves are transforming me. As I walk with the people of Haiti, God continues to transform my life into the person that He created me to be. I pray that, as you read this story, He will transform you as well.

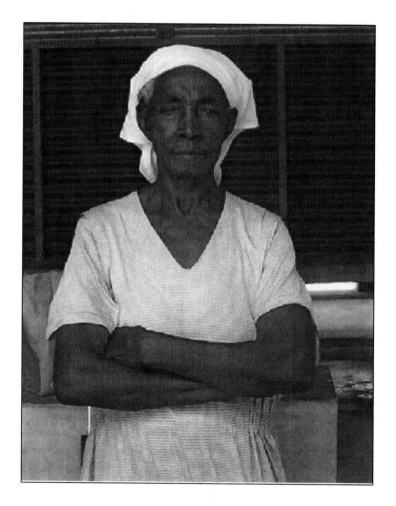

CHAPTER TWO

A matter of perspective...

"Whatever you did for one of the least of these brothers of mine,
you did for me"'
Matthew 25:40 (NIV)

A bar of soap, a cloth diaper, $5, a bottle of Tylenol... all things that are quite small and for the most part, insignificant in our lives here. Yet in another situation they become items of extreme importance.

You see, in the slum where we work in Haiti, clean water is at a premium and must be paid for and hauled on your head in 5 gallon buckets that weigh 40 pounds. Soap, when it is available, which is not often, and clean water are used to wash clothes, and then the wash water is reused to rinse the clothes with. The water may be used again and again to wash more clothes and bodies.

An infant I am seeing in the clinic urinates on my lap while I am examining her. When I investigate, I see it is because she has no diaper on. Her mother simply doesn't have any. In an area where dysentery runs rampant, lack of a simple diaper proves to be a serious concern. Other infants have underwear that is made for toddlers or school age children, thankful to have something.

Many people carry heavy loads on their heads out of necessity and suffer neck pain or chronic headaches as a result. But they endure these with no relief because they have no money for food, much less medication.

Things that are incidentals to us become critical parts of one's life when the need exists and they are not available. That is the way of life in Haiti. Everything becomes a matter of perspective.

I can illustrate this in a more personal way. As a nurse for nearly 25 years, I have helped many an ill patient to the bathroom without really a second thought. It wasn't the most challenging thing I did all day, but a necessary part of the job and I like to think I did it cheerfully (most of the time). Yet three years ago, when I found myself in a hospital bed in the position of needing someone to help me to the bathroom, that person became the most important person in my life for that moment.

It is all a matter of perspective. A young Haitian Bible college student we know had to withdraw from school beginning in January because he lacked the money to pay for his transportation to the school. When we inquired as to how much it was, we were shocked to find out it was only $5 per week. This young student had stopped school because he didn't have $5 per week. I spend more than that each week on gourmet coffee!

I have been so blessed to see how the body of Christ has shown it's faithfulness to the Master as we have made needs like these known. 50 mothers in Haiti had the basic necessities to care for their infants because a group of women in a bible study, a senior citizens Sunday school class and a few colleagues who knew of my work in Haiti have been faithful to the calling of Christ in making up infant care packages to distribute. These packets contained small things-things we would overlook- sippy cups, a few diapers, diaper pins, powder and cream.

Children in a remote village in the mountains who live in an orphanage run by two dedicated and loving nuns had vitamins and distractions for the summer because children in a Sunday school class faithfully made care packages for their Haitian counterparts to use during the summer school recess. A hospital we support and the Christ's Church Clinic were blessed with 5 new microscopes because a dear friend was faithful to God's calling to help the poor and recycled used equipment.

Because of the faithfulness of many people, nearly $5000 worth of medications were purchased to provide assistance to the people of Christ's Church Clinic patients and a clinic we did in a rural mountain village, where no medical care currently exists. Our team ran out of medications one year. That was painful. It was hard enough to try to help people with so little resources, but when we ran out of what we had, the team was completely demoralized. Seeing people in the clinic line and knowing we would have to turn them away because we ran out of medication was exceptionally difficult.

But that didn't happen again because people heard the call and were obedient as we serve in their place in Haiti. Anemic patients will receive all the iron and antibiotic therapy they need because a faithful saint spent countless hours repackaging pills so we could take more of them in less space.

One particular year, late in our preparation I was made aware of an urgent need by the nuns in the mountain village for diapers and formula for a mother of newborn triplets in the rural mountain village. It was a miracle that triplets were born and all three survived at all much less to have to worry about caring for them. I didn't know how I would meet this need because our funds were nearly all designated or spent and formula is very expensive. But the very next day, I received a sizable donation from a couple in our church that felt led to contribute money to the trip. This money went a long way toward providing food for 3 new members of this family. It was a direct answer to prayer.

I was telling a friend recently about one of my Haitian friends who longs to be married. He and his fiancé have been together for 10 years now but they cannot afford to get married because they needed the money to pay for their first years rent in their home once they were married.

As I talked to her, I shared how sad my heart was that people had to put off such an important event in their life sometimes for many, many years simply because they couldn't afford to live together. It was just one of the saddest things I felt as I empathized for my Haitian friend. He wasn't the only one I knew like this. Young people all over Haiti have lengthy engagements due to the lack of finances needed to set up even the most modest housekeeping.

As my friend listened to me recount his story, she asked me "Just how much does it take to pay a years rent in Haiti so they could get married?"

"About $400 is needed for the years rent. He has some of it saved but not nearly enough. I had sent a little for an early wedding present but he is still very short", I replied.

"Well, I will just write you out a check right now for the whole $400 and they can make the plans to get married," she replied.

Suddenly I felt very uncomfortable. I realized it might have seemed like I was fishing for the money when really I was just telling my friend how very sad this situation was.

"Why don't you think about this for a few days and if you still feel that way, you can give us the money then?" I said.

"No", my friend replied, with tears in her eyes. "It isn't often you can help to fix a situation for something as little as $400. I want to do it now", she continued as she got her checkbook out.

And she was right. How often can we really "fix" something by purchasing some soap, buying some vitamins, or giving $400 to cover a whole year of rent for a young married couple desiring to remain pure until they were married?

Don't get me wrong. It will take a lot more that $400 to fix Haiti. Certainly giving money sometimes can be the wrong thing to do. Helping people who are mired in a political struggle which has resulted in poverty, disease and lack of infrastructure is an exceedingly complicated thing to try to deal with effectively.

But giving the $400 was a start. And so for this young man it did start him on a path which was a beginning. He was able to get married. We were able to help by providing him with a job assisting us in our work in Haiti. Providing him with a job helped maintain a sense of self worth. It allows a person to feel more in control of their own situation, more self reliant. It wasn't a perfect system but it was a start.

Things which are so simple, relatively meaningless to us, become things of great value and importance when placed in the context of the people of Haiti. For what I spend on gourmet coffee each week, a young Haitian student can continue his studies to become a minister of God. For what I spent on music downloads for my MP3 player last year, a young mother could obtain vaccinations for her children.

Every prayer that you pray on our behalf will serve to strengthen us, physically and spiritually as we serve thus strengthening the people of Haiti. Your prayers help them minister to us. Your prayers help us keep our hearts tender to the Holy Spirit as we see strength of faith in the presence of evil and desolation. This strength is exemplified by our Lord Himself. Every bar of soap, pair of used glasses, bottle of vitamins, used medication bottles, and piece of children's clothing *will make a difference* to the person in Haiti who will be the recipient.

I know because my eyes have seen it and my heart has felt it. I have received the hug in your place from the woman who is so grateful to get a bottle of ibuprofen for her fever of 104. I have seen the mother weep tears because we were able to help her child's cough resolve. I have cried and prayed with the young woman who needed to get a breast mass biopsied but couldn't because she had no money to go to the local hospital until we assisted her with it.

Each of us must be faithful to God's calling. NOTHING is too small. Not everyone can or should make the trip to Haiti. But each of us is called by Christ Himself to be involved in ministering to the poor and evangelizing the unsaved in some way.

I hope that prayer letters from other missionaries will resonate with you more because you have been a part of a mission experience either by reading this book, going or supporting someone who did. It is my hope that your prayers will be more diligent for them because you have prayed for Haiti. I hope that you will give more liberally to missions in general because you have seen what your gifts might do in Haiti.

$5 made the difference to the Bible college student. The diapers will make a difference to the young Haitian mother. Tylenol is a welcome relief to the Haitian who carries 6 chairs at a time on his head to sell in the market. Small or insignificant things to us, but lifesavers to these precious people who have so little. It is all a matter of perspective.

"Every heart that doesn't know Jesus is a mission field.
Every heart that knows Jesus is a missionary."
Pastor Auguste
Christ's Church of the City, Haiti

CHAPTER THREE

My name is Remy
(M' rele Remy)

"...a real friend sticks closer than a brother."
Proverbs 18:24 (NLT)

"Good morning. My name is Remy."
It was with these words that my life was changed. I had entered the clinic building where we were to see patients the first day of our adventure in Haiti. A young Haitian entered and introduced himself as Remy. He was to be my translator this week. He was small of stature, but I would soon find out his heart was huge.

As we began our work together, my initial impressions of him were that he was very capable and personable. He spoke fluent English. He asked the questions which I asked and in turn, told me the patients response. I was impressed that he didn't seem the least bit uncomfortable with the medical terminology that I used with him.

As the days passed, I grew quite fond of Remy. We worked well together. He exuded a spirit of meekness and confidence. He spoke to the patients in a sensitive, caring manner. It was clear that he was talking to them from his heart and not just using my words. I truly appreciated that since, because of the language barrier, it was difficult for me to speak my heart to them. He translated for me in the most difficult experience I had in Haiti, that of telling a woman she was to die soon, maybe even that very day. He helped me ask her if she knew Jesus (which she did) and then pray with her for a peaceful and merciful homegoing. He was of great comfort to me as we had to leave her likely to die that day.

We found a few things to laugh at-one of which was my poor attempts to speak Haitian Kreyol to the patients, simple things such as just introducing myself to them. Finally, in a sensitive and tactful way, he told me that it might be better if he spoke to them, because they really couldn't understand what I was trying to say. We did laugh together and I took his advice.

I was to learn that he had aspirations of going to the United States to attend college and then medical school. He wanted to be a doctor and return to Haiti to help his people in providing medical care. He also wanted to marry and have children. As the days passed, I had great joy in teaching him some small medical things that I thought might be of interest to him as we saw patients with interesting diseases. He looked in patients ears with me and listened to lungs, among other things.

The final afternoon of our clinic, I needed to stop sometime in the mid-afternoon just to take a short break because the heat was quite oppressive. Remy felt the same way. I took this opportunity to talk to him about his life in Haiti.

We had rarely had time to talk about anything that didn't relate to the patients we were seeing. He told me that he was one of 9 children in his family. They lived in 2 rooms, a 15 minute walk from the church complex at Christ's Church of the City where we were working. They had no electricity, running water, plumbing, toilets or refrigeration. They ate one meal per day and there were days, sometimes as often as every other day, when they didn't eat at all.

As he said this, without missing a beat he added, "But God is good to us. He takes care of my family".

His statement of great faith ministered to me in a way that nothing else had to that point. Through this young Haitian, I came to realize just how much God cares for his children. He watches out for the sparrows and He was watching out for this family that had limited resources in a way that I could not understand. Because he had to rely on God for literally every little thing in his life, including food and shelter, Remy had developed a great faith. Yet there was no alarm in his statement, just great faith. He told me how God has kept him and his family though difficult times. He had given him the vision of being a doctor and God had allowed him to work with his pastor who became his mentor.

I, like many others on my team, assumed that those who worked with us in the clinic were somehow not like the people who came for treatment—that they were more fortunate than the poor, hungry, ill people that came for treatment. But we came to realize that the people who were sitting next to us were no different. A difficult lesson, but one we needed to learn.

On the last day that we worked together in the clinic, I scribbled a note to him at lunch time on a scrap piece of paper which I found laying around. I told him how much I appreciated his efforts at helping me see the patients and how he had impressed me with both his attitude and spirit. God clearly was going to use him for a great purpose in His kingdom. I wanted him to know how my life had been changed by his simple yet great faith. I ended the note with a sentiment that if we never met again in our earthly home, I knew that I would see him again in our heavenly home. I left him with the scripture that I claimed for that week, Acts 20:24, "If only I may finish the race and complete the task the Lord Jesus has given me-the task of testifying to the gospel of God's grace". (NIV)

As we left that day, I had tears in my eyes. He told me I had changed his life. But if that were the case, it was only a fraction of the way he had changed mine. This young Haitian had taught me many lessons that week. He taught me again to be sensitive to those directly around us, not to miss the needs of those most near us, sitting next to, behind and in front of us, simply because they are familiar to us. He taught me what it is like to believe in God for the most fundamental things in life and how our faith will grow as a result. He also taught me what it means to love-love the patients that he spoke with sensitively, love the Lord in a simple yet so profound way, and to love others, like myself, by serving with and by them.

That was only to be the beginning of a relationship which I would come to treasure in a way that is difficult to speak of. Remy and I have become very good friends during the years I have worked in Haiti. You will read much about him in the pages which follow.

We have seen each other through the most difficult of times. The summer after we first met, Remy received a full scholarship to attend college in the United States. His dream was to become a physician and return to Haiti to care for those who had no access to medical care. He had a vision of being a physician who would travel from village to village providing medical care to those who lived in rural and unserved areas of Haiti.

Several months later, however when the time came to get his visa, he was denied a student visa by the US State Department. This is a common problem for many Haitians. The US government is very sensitive to the problem of illegal immigration by people of developing countries. Haitians have it especially difficult. The government is concerned that, given the level of poverty and problems in Haiti, once a person gets into this country they will have little incentive to return and thus may illegally stay.

This was devastating to Remy. His dream to become a physician and provide for his family had just been dashed. It was a difficult time for him and for me as I saw how his heart was broken. He tried to explain to the US officials that he would return to Haiti but to no avail.

Over the next year, we looked at options for Remy to achieve his dream. With much work and effort on both our parts, he applied and was accepted to a Haitian medical school. He is over half way through his training now. He is working hard in Haiti studying and I am working hard on his behalf here raising the financial support for his education. He still has the dream of working in the small villages of Haiti giving medical care to the poor there. We are dreaming a dream together of starting a mobile clinic where we would both work together in serving the medical needs of the rural poor in Haiti.

Since the day that I met Remy, God has shown me so many things through our friendship. My life was changed by him. Few people on my journey have had the profound effect on me that he did. I remember a very special breast cancer patient who taught me the meaning of courage in the face of death. I can think of a friend who triumphed over great adversity and was a real inspiration. And for those difficult experiences, my life was and continues to be enriched.

But the Lord used Remy to teach me many lessons that first week in Haiti. He was a precious gift to me from the Father—for in him I found embodied the sentiment of the Haitian Christians-simple faith and love for the Lord our God in any circumstances. I can pray more effectively for the Haitians and the poor all over the world, because I know one of them now. He represents them to me. Because of that, I can represent them to the Father.

M' rele Remy.

CHAPTER FOUR

A Lesson Before Dying

"...I was sick and you looked after me..."
Matthew 25:35 (NIV)

This is a difficult story to tell. It took me nearly 2 months to be able to understand fully enough what God was trying to tell me through this experience to put it on paper. But it is one that needs to be told. It is a story of humility, grace, redemption and God's ultimate glory.

It was Thursday, May 3, 2001. The day before had been our first day in the clinic at Christ's Church of the City. It had been eye opening, but we all knew better what we were dealing with (or so we thought). At least this day we came a little more prepared to meet the challenges of administering rudimentary but needed medical care to the people of this urban slum in Haiti-the poorest slum in the western Hemisphere.

It was 7:50AM. I had just entered the clinic and had put my water bottle, stethoscope and camera down on the table. Our Haitian host pastor entered my room and with urgency in his voice, asked me to come outside to see a woman immediately. He wanted to know if we could do anything to help her.

I grabbed my translator, Remy-my lifeline for that week, soon to become a dear friend- and told him we needed to go outside. We exited the clinic through the same door I had just entered. I had seen the hundreds of people waiting in line as we entered and even spoke to some of them.

There are no appointment times in Haiti. Everyone shows up at the crack of dawn and all wait-for the most part patiently-until their turn in line to see the "doktor". Quite a difference from our own culture where waiting even 5 minutes can lead to pacing or annoyance.

As I had entered, I hadn't noticed anything out of the ordinary. However, as we turned the corner, our host pastor pointed to a young woman, maybe in her early 20's, lying on a straw mat on the ground, leaning against the knees of the young man with her. From where I was, it looked like she might be very pregnant. She was quite thin-there are no overweight Haitians, but she was much thinner than most-making her abdomen look even larger.

As I approached her, it became apparent very quickly to me what the problem was. She opened her eyes to reveal very jaundiced sclera (the whites of ones eyes). Those, along with her distended belly, were the telltale signs of end stage liver failure. Given her age, I guessed that she had hepatitis, cancer or AIDS.

I had been told that our host carefully screens the patients that we see in the clinic. He tries to see that very severely ill patients are not brought to the clinic. This is painful but necessary for a couple of very good reasons.

First, our resources are very limited there and it is impossible to treat very sick patients. But, more importantly, were a patient to die at the clinic when the Americans were there giving medical care, his reputation in the community could be damaged. There is a large amount of superstition in Haiti. Belief in the spirit world infiltrates every area of the culture. One could think that there were evil spirits here if someone died. That would be devastating to the ministry.

The clinic is also designed to be a spiritual outreach of the church to the people of this slum and he does not want to risk anything that would make the church or the Americans unwelcome in the community. This is only one of many very hard decisions that need to be made in Haiti. So while it is not a job I would envy doing, I understood his concern when he saw this woman waiting there. However, he had true compassion for her and desired her to be cared for if it was possible.

I knelt down on the gravel yard where she was waiting and, through my translator, asked her some cursory questions. But they were really not necessary. It was very apparent to me that this young woman was dying. And her death was very near. Although she denied acute pain, her abdomen was so distended that she was having trouble breathing.

I had seen many patients like this before and I knew there was nothing medically we could do for her with the resources we had available to us. I considered seeing if we could do a paracentesis-a small procedure where a needle and syringe are used to withdraw the fluid in the abdomen to make the patient more comfortable and breathing easier. However, we were not set up to do it and in retrospect it would have been too risky to do anyway-it may have even caused her immediate death.

Remy and I went to find our host. I told him we could not treat her medically, but I offered to pray with her and give her what we had for pain before he sent them away. He agreed. Knowing this would be a difficult thing for us, I grabbed the first team member I saw and it happened to be Shelia, my best friend who was on the trip also. I took her by both hands and explained that we were going to have to go pray with a young woman outside who was dying. We took deep breaths, breathed a prayer for ourselves and followed our translator outside.

We all knelt down on the ground. Through Remy, I did the most difficult thing I did in Haiti all week. I told this young woman she was dying and that her death was very close, maybe even this day. She said she understood. I asked her if she knew Jesus and she responded affirmatively. Through Remy, I asked her if she had asked the Lord to forgive her of her sins and if she knew for certain that she would go to be with Him in heaven when she died. She nodded her head, yes.

I told her that there were no medicines we had there that could help her and that we could offer her nothing in the way of medical care except for some pain medicine. Her condition was far too advanced. But, I told her that we wanted to pray with and for her before she left. She readily agreed.

We gathered around her, the 3 of us, in a small circle to pray with her. As we did this, an amazing thing happened. The people who were sitting in lines around her, spontaneously, stood up and formed a circle surrounding us. Shelia, Remy and I all laid our hands on this precious child of God.

At that moment, I felt a sensation like one I have never felt before-a tremendous Presence that is indescribable. As we touched her dying body, she used much of her remaining strength to raise her hands heavenward. Through a stream of tears, I prayed a prayer thanking God for her young life and asking for His gracious peace in her homegoing. I prayed for His mercy to make her remaining time short, without undue pain and to bring her to Him very soon. When I finished, we all hugged her and left to go back into the clinic. Shelia and I held each other for a moment, she returned to the clinic lobby. I returned to my room with Remy. It was a powerful experience.

I wasn't exactly sure what had just happened, but we needed to go on-the second most difficult thing I did in Haiti that week. I told Remy that I needed a minute to compose myself and he suggested that we pray together, which we did. He was a gift from God to me in that experience. For that I was very grateful. After we prayed for strength to continue, I wiped my tears and went on to see the first patient I was to see that day. I walked outside a couple of hours later to see that she was gone.

There were so many images and sensations that week in Haiti that I could not fully understand what had happened that day until weeks later. When Shelia and I were talking about it we both came to the same conclusion. We are convinced that the Presence we felt with her that day was God's spirit ministering to us as we ministered to her-maybe through His angels.

In my minds eye, I can see the scene now-the 3 of us gathered around her, perhaps she was even raising her hands to welcome them. They were there, hovering over us, many wings covering us, protecting us and giving us the strength and presence of God that this young woman needed at this critical moment in her life.

I have heard people describe experiences like this but, until that day, I have never experienced it myself. It was a very difficult experience but one that I feel very privileged to have been called to participate in. Remy, Shelia and I were likely the last persons on this earth to invoke the spirit of God in this woman's life and it was in the presence of His angels.

I have seen many patients like this young woman. Having worked in the cancer center at Duke for 7 years, many people presented to our clinic in the same way that she did. So I was not surprised by her condition. I have also attended a number of deaths of patients, friends and relatives, so dealing with the dying is not new to me either. It is never easy, but I am experienced in it.

Yet seeing this young woman dying in this crudest of all situations, lying on the ground no less, knowing that I was totally helpless and completely dependant on God for anything I could offer her, was a deeply humbling experience and one I will NEVER forget.

But, God, in His grace, has placed islands of hope in this vast sea of human misery and suffering. We just have to open our eyes to see them. There is an infant in Haiti who is alive today, who wouldn't be, had it not been for the diligent care and treatment of several people in seeing that he got antibiotics and rehydration over the 3 days we were there. There is a baby in this most horrible slum with severe second and third degree burns that are less likely to be infected because two young women, a nurse and a physical therapist tediously dressed his wounds, sacrificing their own drinking water, the only clean water available, to help remove the old bandages and cleanse his wounds.

There is a woman who lives in an isolated shack in the mountains, who was too ill and weak to come to the clinic on her own who is now recovering from severe pneumonia because a doctor and several helpers hiked to her home 2 hours from the clinic through rugged mountain paths to make a hut call, to treat her and 2 others on the way.

And there is a woman sitting with our Master in Glory, whose homegoing, hopefully, was easier because we ministered to her in Jesus name that day.

I started this story by quoting Jesus, in Matthew 25 as He helped his disciples understand what is meant when He instructed them to serve the poor, the sick, the lost, the lonely, the prisoners, the lost and forgotten.

I hope this is what He would have said to us after that trip: —

"My Child," you ask, "when did you see me? You saw me when I lived in Haiti and you came there to help me. I was the baby with bad burns; you tirelessly took 2 hours to dress my wounds and sang to me as you did it. I was the infant with pneumonia and you developed a solution from what you had to give me fluid and medicine. I was weak, alone, unable to come to you to receive care and you walked to me on hard paths. I was the young woman dying and you prayed for mercy and peace for me at the end of my journey here."

May God always find us faithful.

Photograph by Terry Simpson. © 2003.
Used with permission

CHAPTER FIVE

To Suffer with Others...

Do nothing out of selfish ambition or vain conceit but in humility consider others better than yourselves. Each of you should look not only to your own interests but also to the interests of others. Your attitude should be the same as that of Christ Jesus, who being in the very nature God, did not consider quality with God something to be grasped but made himself nothing, taking the very nature of a servant, being made in human likeness. And being found in appearance like a man, he humbled himself and became obedient to death, even death on a cross. Therefore God exalted Him to the highest place and gave him the name that is above every name, that at the name of Jesus every knee should bow in heaven and earth and every tongue confess that Jesus Christ is Lord to the glory of God the Father.
Philippians 2: 3-11. (NIV)

The word compassion is derived from the Latin word that means, "to suffer with". Compassion asks us to go where it hurts, to enter places of pain, to share in brokenness, fear, confusion and anguish. Compassion challenges us to cry out with those in misery, to mourn with those who are lonely, to weep with those in tears. Compassion requires us to be weak with the weak, vulnerable with the vulnerable and powerless with the powerless. Compassion means full immersion in the condition of being human. Compassion is more than just a general kindness or tenderheartedness (Nouwen; Compassion: A Reflection on the Christian life). If we are to truly show compassion, we must get down to where people are hurting, not stand on the periphery.

Compassion doesn't require us to provide answers to life's complex problems or to explain the "whys" of the difficulties we are asked to endure. It requires us to BE with each other. It means we must practice the power of presence.

Yet compassion is not something that comes naturally to us. Our natural inclination is to avoid the difficulty that comes into our own lives, much less enter into the difficulties of others. We see hardships, problems, trials, loss and pain as things to be avoided. As Paul states clearly in the Philippians passage, that is not the example that Jesus gave us to follow. He gave up being God to meet us where we are. Perhaps we should see trials and problems as things into which we should immerse ourselves.

How often have we avoided a difficult situation because we didn't know the right words to say or we couldn't offer some sort of reasonable explanation or word of comfort which might ease the pain in some way?

There are no easy answers to what you will see in Haiti. There may be no answers at all to some things that we see. But sharing in the suffering by offering something as simple as your presence is what we are called to do.

God has called us to have compassion for, and thus to suffer with, these people. We see much suffering in Haiti. You can't look away from it. It will surround you everywhere you go. In addition to the deep human suffering you will see, you will also see God's grace as you have never seen it before.

God is in Haiti. There is no doubt about it. He has given these people an overflowing measure of His grace to meet the circumstances in which they find themselves.

Regardless of your gift or experiences, we will each have many opportunities "to suffer with" others if we choose to. Just practicing the power of presence with those less fortunate materially than ourselves is the first step. Being willing just to "be with" people- that is what is required.

My third trip to Haiti, my dear friend Remy asked me to visit his home one day. I was deeply honored to do that. I had driven down the streets of this slum many times and knew how people lived there. Remy had described how he lived and my heart was saddened by it. Yet, I had remained at a distance.

He took me to a part of the slum area I have never been. The area outside the church is a "commercial" area. There are many street vendors outside the walls of the complex. In their makeshift stands, they are selling most anything that people would need. While we drove by houses on the way in, I had never seen one up close or been in one.

As we approached his home, we drove over one of the many cement canals in the landfill that people there call home. Many years before, these had originally been built to drain the water away from the city during torrential rains that characterize the rainy season in Haiti. However, in the many years since, they had come to serve the purpose of a place to dispose of garbage. Scattered throughout the city, most of them were nearly full of garbage. This one was no different. What water is able to drain eventually overflows the canal banks leading to the flooding that it was intended to prevent. Only now along with the water, the streets are also flooded with trash.

We neared a small cluster of cement block homes. They were all attached to each other in a similar fashion to our townhouses. They were very small. All had some sort of iron bars over the porches and any windows.

We pulled off the road and parked. He led me through a larger iron gate into what looked like a large alley lined with these small cement "townhouses". When we arrived at Remy's home, his family was waiting for us. He had told them I was coming. For a reason I didn't understand, he seemed nervous. On the other hand, I was quite excited at the possibility of seeing his home and meeting all of his family.

As I entered the dark home, I came into one of the two rooms which housed this family of 12 people. It had a twin bed in it which doubled as a couch when needed for that purpose. A small wooden shelving unit held a number of small knick knacks. There was a single iron chair there which was offered to me.

I felt strange sitting there with everyone else standing around me. I was to learn that it was the Haitian custom to offer the guest a seat. So I took it. I would be the recipient of this custom often in Haiti. We talked for a few minutes as I met his brothers and sisters.

When he asked me if I would like to see the rest of the home, I said "Yes if it wasn't too much trouble."

The second room, about the same size- maybe 10 x 10- and had a double bed in it and a small dresser. Through that room was a door leading behind the house. Out the back door was a small dirt area with a hole in the ground about two feet by two feet covered by a cement lid. This was their latrine, he informed me. In the corner of the back yard stood the tiniest palm tree. It was about three feet tall and by the attention paid to it, it was clearly a treasure of which his family was very proud. There wasn't much green in the slum area.

Remy seemed nervous and rushed me around this quick tour. Abruptly, after about 10 minutes he told me it was time to go and we had to leave. We walked the block or so to the truck and got in to return to the guest house.

I mentioned to him on the ride back that I wished I could have stayed longer. He explained to me that he didn't want me to. He was worried that if his neighbors saw a "blan" (a white person) coming to his home, they would think I had given them money. Most all Haitians associated Caucasians with having lots of money. While we do have much when compared to them, most of us are far from what we would consider rich. But in Haiti, any Caucasian is considered rich. He was afraid that his family would be targeted for robbery because if anyone in the community had seen me come to their home they would assume there was now money in the house.

I later learned that he had sat up all night watching the door for signs of an intruder. My attempt to put myself into the world of my friend had actually put him and his family in jeopardy. These kinds of paradoxes are around every corner in Haiti. As I tried to show my willingness to be with them in their world, I had unknowingly put them in danger. But it was what they had wanted. I have found that risks are just part and parcel of everyday life in Haiti. They take risks like this every day and really have no choice about whether to take them or not.

It was not until I actually entered into his world, stepped out of the protected compound of my world, saw with my own eyes, sit where he sits, walk where he walks each day and allowed myself to "suffer with him" in this smallest of ways, that I began to really understand what it means to live in this poor slum in Haiti. Isn't that what Jesus did for us? He came to where we are and walked our daily walk.

That night, I cried in my bed at the guest house for my dear friend living in the squalor that I had witnessed that day. My heart ached thinking of people being proud of such a small sign of the beauty of God's creation as that little palm tree. And the latrine....it was just too much to think about. The fact that they had risked potential danger to invite me to their home was nearly more than I could bear.

I asked God why these kind of things need to exist. He revealed to me that we are fallen and as long as sin is in this world, we will have injustice, poverty and pain. But He can and will help us overcome it through the power of His love. Entering into this suffering is to share in the cross of Jesus Christ and is one of the ways we can help with the solution. .

It is painful to suffer with others. But as we view difficulties and trials more as a part of our Christian life and less as something to be avoided that we truly grow to be more like the Christ who made Himself man for us. Part of the pain of suffering is our innate nature to avoid it. Avoidance, in and of itself, is painful. It takes a lot of energy to avoid things.

Once we realize that God uses our compassion and suffering with others to grow us, and decide to embrace it when it comes our way or the way of those we love and care for, it ceases to be as painful. We free up the energy we spent avoiding it, to use engaging in the pain of others. We can focus more directly in seeking God and what He would have us learn in the process of having compassion for others.

Having compassion is a process. I have spent my 25 year career trying to develop a degree of compassion for others. It is difficult. So use the experiences you find yourself in as a part of that process. Embrace suffering and God will honor your efforts.

Seek experiences to suffer with others as you develop your sense of compassion. These will be opportunities God has for each of us to suffer with others. I pray for each of us that we will ask God to open wide the doors of our heart that we might fully experience what He has for us individually as we practice the power presence..

It will be joyous, painful, fun, difficult and challenging. But we will be better people- Christians who are closer to being the humble and obedient servant Paul describes in the passage above. In doing so, don't be surprised if you find yourself being ministered to by the very people that you have chosen "to suffer with". The Haitians are close to God because of their need to have the kind of faith that requires them to rely on God for everything. We have much to learn from them.

Chris Rice put it so well in his song "The Face of Christ:

"How did I found myself in a better place?
I can't look down on the frown in the other guy's face,
'cause when I stoop down low and look him square in the eyes, I
get the funny feeling
I just might be seeing the face of Christ. "[3]

I don't know how I found myself in a "better" place than many of the Haitian friends I have come to love deeply. I don't even know if my place is a "better" place. Sure, I have money and enough food to eat, a house to live and a job. But there are so many distractions here to keep God from entering fully into my life.

But I do know that as I have allowed myself to be with the Haitians, to look them squarely in the eyes, to have compassion for them, to fully suffer with them, I have seen the very face of Christ. And my life will never be the same. But it requires work. And we can't do it from where we are; we must "stoop down low".

CHAPTER SIX

The Gift

*"A gift opens the way for the giver
and ushers him into the presence of the great."*
Proverbs 18:16 (NIV)

This trip to Haiti had been troubled from September 11, 2001 onward. It was scheduled for October, 2001. Because of concerns for personal safety as they related to the recent terrorist attack on the World Trade Center and its aftermath, a number of people had decided not to go. The trip nearly didn't happen because of generalized concern of the remaining team members. But those of us who were willing did board the plane on October 6, 2001 and took off for Port au Prince Haiti. I know I wasn't the only one who left loved ones in tears, concerned for our safety.

Because of the lack of personnel, the clinic had not functioned as it normally would. Fewer providers were available to see patients and less support people were there to assist. But we were very "Haitian" and did what we could with the resources we had. Ultimately, we did quite a bit, much more than would have occurred had we not come.

On the last day of clinic, we were packing up readying to leave at noon to do some sight seeing and shopping before returning to the United States the next morning. I was sitting in my room tying up some final paperwork, when Remy entered my room and sat down on the bench beside my chair.

Remy is a dear friend who served as my translator on my first trip to Haiti. We became fast friends thanks to email. Both of us were excited when I made the decision to return in October. We had not gotten to see each other as much during this week as we both had hoped. But we did spend time together each day at lunch and before returning to the guesthouse in the evening.

I noticed then that Remy had closed the door as he entered, but didn't really think much of that. As I turned to him, I also noticed he carried a white plastic grocery bag in his hand.

He handed me the bag and said, "This is for you".

Since my mind was focused on what I was tending to, I assumed that the contents of the bag contained more things for me to pack up. Consequently, I took the bag and held it on my lap while I finished writing my final notes.

When I looked over at Remy a minute or so later, he sat there waiting patiently for me to look in the bag. My thoughts were still on other things, so as I opened the bag and felt the contents quite heavy, I wondered what this was.

Inside the bag was a beautiful, hand carved, mahogany box-the kind that are frequently seen on the sides of most Haitian roads where there are street vendors present and in the local markets. I realized then just what this was. The contents of the bag were not medications or supplies that needed to be packed. What this bag contained was a precious gift from my friend to me.

I can only imagine what my face must have looked like when I realized that I had just been the recipient of such a gift.

I turned to Remy and said the only thing I could think to say immediately, "Remy, I don't want you spending your money on gifts for me."

His response is one I will never forget.

He said, "But... you must accept it."

The reality of the situation I was in the midst of hit me immediately. All I could do to express the myriad of intense feelings I was experiencing was to weep openly. I couldn't speak. I couldn't move. I could only sob with my head in my hands, while

I felt Remy's hand on my shoulder. When I finally composed myself-literally several minutes later-I hugged Remy and thanked him for the lovely gift. I, then, assured him that of course, I would accept it.

We were in the final minutes of preparing to leave and I knew I had to complete my work. But at that point in time, NOTHING was as important to me as this moment. No schedule, no time frame, no packing duties, NOTHING.

A favorite song says "We have this moment to hold in our hands and to touch as it slips through our fingers like sand." [4]

The Lord quietly spoke to me and said, "This moment is my gift to you. Take from it all you can".

I was determined to get every little grain of sand out of this moment. I would realize later that this moment was one that would literally change my life.

I tried quite inadequately, I'm afraid, to thank Remy for the lovely gift. I couldn't tell him this at that time, but I would write to him later, that it is the most precious gift I have ever received. Because of that, his gift is one I would cherish forever. I am not sure he really understood the intensity of my feelings about this precious gift. It would take me the rest of the day to sort through what the Lord was trying to tell me.

This is the message I received from the Lord. There are 2 very specific times in my life where a spiritual teaching that I have believed my entire life has been made so crystal clear to me, that I felt God was standing right there in front of me speaking to me. The first one was on Palm Sunday, 1995. Instead of preaching as we are used to him doing, my pastor at the time, Ed Henagar, simply recited the passage of scripture from Matthew 23-25 which dealt with the final hours of Jesus' life before his crucifixion on the cross. Just listening as the scripture was presented in Ed's wonderful bass voice, with no commentary or practical applications mentioned, just the Word of God, was a powerful thing.

I had heard the story of Good Friday ever since I was old enough to go to Sunday school. I believed it all. But it was on that Sunday morning that the mental and physical anguish, agony and torture that our Savior endured on my behalf prior to ultimately sacrificing His life for me became so very real to me. It is a Sunday morning I will never forget.

The other time was this day. As we prepared to say good bye, I asked Remy if I could pray with him before leaving. Our hands found each other and we bowed our heads in prayer. I felt the Holy Spirit in the room with us. The time of prayer we had together is difficult to explain, but clearly God's spirit was there, interceding to the heavenly throne for us in a supernatural way.

The good-byes were very difficult and my tears were still flowing. But it was in the tap-tap (a Haitian version of a taxi), driving up the mountain road, that I realized why this gift had elicited such powerful feelings.

Because I had come to know Remy well over the last 6 months, I knew what his life was like. I knew that he did not "manje chak jou"-eat every day. I knew that he lived in a house with 2 rooms and 10 siblings, with no plumbing, electricity, toilets, running water and little to no food.

I knew that he had made $12 each day he had translated for us. Translating for the missionaries is considered a highly skilled job. Unskilled manual laborers are lucky to get $1 per day for desperately hard work in the hot Haitian sun. He would probably spend the money he earned this week paying for schooling for his younger brother and sister.

I knew that he didn't know when the next time would be that he would be able to earn some money. I knew that he was very anemic and did not have the resources to eat what was needed to remedy that situation.

But most of all, I knew that he had used money that would buy food for him and his family to purchase this gift for me. It was this revelation that pierced through my heart that morning. He had SACRIFICED for me.

I must say that in my life, I can think of no real time when I have "sacrificed". There have been times when I did without some things so that I could have others. I feel sure that early in their life together, my parents did sacrifice in this way for their family. But my life has been such that sacrifice has been a concept I understand, appreciate and would do (I hope), should it become necessary, but not one I can really say I have experienced.

Sitting there in front of me that Friday morning, in the poorest slum in the Western Hemisphere, was a friend who had sacrificed something very dear for me— food for his stomach.

I realized through the situation I had just experienced that this is exactly how we often respond to God. He presents us with His gift, we make Him sit there and wait until we are finished with what we deem as important at that time. When He offers us His gift, we tell Him it is too valuable for us to accept and we are not worthy.

Yet He says exactly what Remy said to me, "YOU MUST ACCEPT THIS."

Remy had not given up something easy like a new pair of shoes for a special event, or a trip that one wants to take. No, he had given up food for his hungry stomach to buy me this gift.

It was at this time that I knew what God was telling me through this humble servant of His. It was so clear that, as we rode through the dusty streets of Port au Prince, I felt like our Lord and Savior was sitting right there beside me in the tap-tap—just like that Palm Sunday morning at Blacknall Presbyterian Church in 1995.

It was as if He was saying to me, "Yes, my servant and beloved child Remy loves you so much that he willingly gave up food to buy you this lovely gift. And you value his love for you a great deal because of that. But I love you so much more than Remy does. I love you so much I gave up my life so you would come to love me as much as I love you. I didn't give up food needed for my physical sustenance; I gave up my life for you. Free, and complete, for you. And I would have done it had you been the only one who needed it. I love you this much, April."

The sacrifice Remy made to purchase the gift for me was as close as I was going to come in this temporal world we live in to seeing with my own eyes just how costly the sacrifice was that God made in giving us the gift of His son-Jesi Kri (Jesus Christ). And it wasn't just the gift of His son. He sacrificed the life of His son to the forces of evil in this world, through torture and an anguishing death, so that we might come to love Him in the same way He loves us.

Remy's gift to me, the beautiful box, is displayed in a prominent place in my home, a place where I see it many times each day and think of him. I keep my things I take on each trip to Haiti in it. When we have friends over, I bring it down to where we are gathered so that others can see it also. The value of this gift is not in its monetary worth-although, I know that is was not inexpensive, even in Haitian dollars.

The value of this gift for me is twofold. First, it is valuable because my friend was obedient to the Lord in sacrificing so that I might have this gift. But the additional value of this gift is in the message that his action sent to me from our Heavenly Father-that of a love that will never let us go; a love that will be there for us always; a love that was paid for with a very dear price on the cross on another hot Friday afternoon on a hill called Mount Calvary over 2000 years ago with the greatest sacrifice ever- the life of the Son of God.

Remy wrote me later that he did not realize I would "appreciate my gift so much". No, I doubt I will ever be able to tell him just what his gift meant to me or how my life was changed forever on that hot Friday afternoon, this time in a slum of Port au Prince, Haiti. I doubt I will ever be able to express to my Heavenly Father what the sacrifice of His son has meant to me.

But I can try.

I can make my life, what the apostle Paul refers to as, a living sacrifice, pure and holy, acceptable and pleasing to God, the love of my life, my Father, Maker, Creator and Friend.

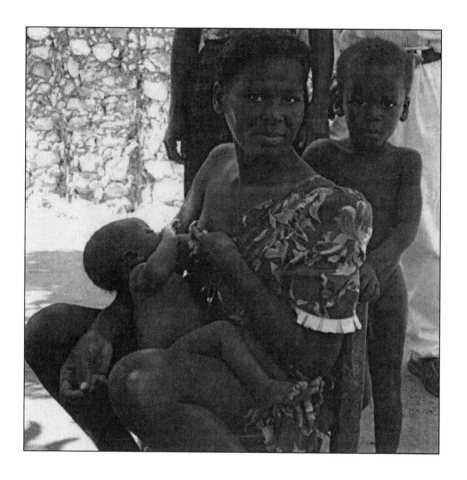

CHAPTER SEVEN

Position Yourself to Receive a Blessing

"Jacob said to his father, "I am Esau your firstborn;
I have done as you told me.
Get up, please, sit and eat of my game, that you may bless me."
Genesis 27:19 (NASB)

"You have put yourself in a position to receive a blessing."
That was what a friend had said to me as I told her of my upcoming travels to Haiti. This was my first trip to Haiti.

I had never thought of it quite like that before. In fact, what I remembered was that when I was asked to go on this trip, the person who asked me preceded the request with-"I know you probably will think twice before you volunteer to go again but could you..."

As I think back on that, I realize that had I thought twice, I might not have "positioned myself to receive the blessing".

Had I taken the time to really realize what was involved, I might have said, "No I don't think so, not this time."

And in essence I would have been saying to God "No I don't think I'll take that blessing this time."

It seems ludicrous to think of responding to God that way, but we do it all the time, maybe daily, sometimes multiple times per day. What a regret that would have been.

Whether we realize it or not, I believe we have all chosen to put ourselves in a position to receive a blessing as we answer the call to serve the poor. Whether that is what we were thinking, regardless of how we got here, we were in that place. We have prepared our meal, just as Jacob did with Isaac, and have delivered it to God in the areas in Haiti where we work. Our motives might have been like Jacob's—deceit, ignorance, selfishness, something else, possibly a combination of all of them. We are after all complicated creatures— as is our Creator.

However, we were there— in the position to get the blessing. And the way we were to get the blessing was to be Jesus to these humble, honorable people. The blessing was ours to receive and it was given to us through these people, the people that we encountered over the next week.

They were blessed as well, through our meager, failing and faltering efforts-efforts like filthy rags. I have enough confidence in the omnipotence of God to take my weak, poor efforts and use them to His glory-He has done it before. He certainly did it that week. The Haitians efforts to bless us were somewhat more refined, even though we found ourselves in this "Third World", they had much to give us.

Jacob deceived Isaac to receive his blessing-no doubt about that- but it was a blessing none the less. God used his sin of deceitfulness, to eventually bring glory to His name, as He has done with so many others- David, Paul, Peter, me, you.

God was waiting to reveal Himself to us, here in this poorest of the poorest slums in Haiti.

God would speak to us, if we would open our ears and listen to hear him.

God would reveal Himself, if we would look around to see Him.

He would bless us if we would position ourselves to receive it.

He would meet us here in Christ's Church of the City, the mountain village, and Port au Prince, Haiti. He was already there. The Holy Spirit had been the advance person for us.

God was there. God was waiting. God was ready to give us the blessing-despite the motives behind our being here. He wanted to bless us.

We just had to respond to Him as urgently as Jacob did, "Yes, I want the blessing."

May we not respond "No, I don't think so, not this time".

He reminds us, "Maybe you'll think twice next time I ask you to go somewhere…"

And then again, maybe we won't think twice.

CHAPTER EIGHT

"If just a cup of water...."

*"And if you give even a cup of cold water to one of
the least of my followers, you will surely be rewarded."*
Matthew 10:42 (NLT)

My office is located directly across from the waiting room in the Pediatric Cardiac Catheterization lab of a major university medical center. As you might imagine, this presents some interesting "opportunities for service." I don't really have any formal contact with these families. I deal with children who have heart diseases in another context. But this is where the Lord located me physically and a number of situations have happened which have opened my eyes both as a professional and a human being. This is one of them.

I usually keep my door open to increase the ventilation. On this particular day, the door was open and there were only two people in the waiting room—a middle-aged woman and her mother. The middle-aged woman's young daughter had a serious heart defect and was in the cath lab undergoing a procedure. The two were talking quietly.

I have learned to tune people out and keep to my work. However, the mother was out in the hall and I heard her telling the grandmother that she would very much like a drink. For some reason, my ears caught this.

I got up from my desk and went out into the hall. She asked me if there was a drink machine in this area. Since there isn't one directly in our area, I explained to her that there was one on this floor on the other side of the hospital, or in the cafeteria on the first floor.

She didn't want to leave the area as she might miss something happening to her daughter. So, forlornly, they turned to go back into the waiting room. Her situation touched my heart and I offered to get her a drink from our personnel lounge which was right next door to my office. As it turned out, she actually had a canned drink in her pocketbook, but it was now room temperature.

Well, that was easy to fix. I had ice available to me in the next room. I told them to sit down and I would bring them some ice. I went to get two cups of ice and returned to the waiting room with it.

As I walked back to my office, I heard the grandmother say, "I wish I could tell that woman just how much this ice means to us..."

Such innocent words. Perhaps unnoticable to many. But they were a profound statement of gratitude from a person in need. To say that I found it difficult to refocus on my work would be a gross understatement. Here at my disposal were all of my finely tuned medical skills, a plethora of high tech equipment and all she needed at that moment in time was a cup of ice.

Because I had overheard her, I DID realize just what that ice meant to those two mothers dealing with a very difficult situation that day. That happened over four years ago. When I remember it, it seems like it was yesterday—it still brings tears to my eyes.

That was the first encounter I really had with the "cup of cold water" method of service to Christ. Many more were to follow as I served Christ in Haiti.

As I have worked to provide medical care in Haiti over the last several years, I have been plagued with questions which have haunted missionaries for decades. All of these concerns can be summed up in the question of:

Given the limited resources-financial, human, and structural and others- what is the most effective way to deliver effective health care to the most people possible who will see real benefits and improve the life situation for Haitians as a whole?

This is obviously a difficult situation but in reality the answer may be easier than one initially thinks. The goal of all mission work, including medical missions, should be to ultimately turn the work over to the nationals. Any mission group, NGO or non profit which does not have a well thought out and defined exit strategy, best serves the indigenous population by rethinking their philosophy. To do otherwise will only begin the cascade of dependency, diminish the self esteem of those we endeavor to serve and ultimately reinforce the negative perception of the "foreign do-gooders" who in the end do little good at all.

Nate Saint, long term missionary to the Auca Indians in South America, tried to explain this to his Auca friends. When asked by local tribal leaders to bring a missionary dentist to them to provide these services, he replied "The only people who are here all the time are you. So if you want these services all the time, you need to learn to provide them for yourselves".

As a health care provider in a highly technical and sophisticated sub specialty, one of the most difficult things for me to learn was to recognize my own limitations in Haiti. It was and remains exceedingly difficult to see a blue baby with a heart murmur in whom I suspect a septal defect (an opening in one of the walls of the chambers of the heart) and know that at home a simple echocardiogram test could yield the diagnostic data we would need to schedule relatively simple corrective surgery. In Haiti there is no access to cardiovascular surgery, much less pediatric heart surgery even for a simple thing like a ventricular septal defect. There is little hope of even getting an echocardiogram. And given that no intervention is available, one would need to ask of what use is the information anyway?

I have come to realize and accept that my skills are better used evaluating what basic population based health problems exist that I might be able to intervene with to make a difference in children's lives across the population. Given that all-cause mortality in children in Haiti is 30% before the age of 5 and that 15% of children die before their first birthday, mostly of preventable diseases, there is clearly much work to do.

An effective medical missionary will evaluate the needs of the indigenous people and the resources that exist with them and see how they can help with those instead of trying to fit their particular skill set into a system which most likely will not accommodate them. While I could use many specialties as examples, I will use my own situation to illustrate this. I could work long and hard to try to bring pediatric cardiovascular diagnostic tools and the facilities to do such surgery to Haiti. Perhaps that may be a worthy endeavor.

But in reality, it seems to me, my energies are better used in other ways. As I have observed the children I have seen in clinics across Haiti, I have concluded that what the children in Haiti need is clean water, vaccinations, adequate vitamin and mineral intake, maternal education regarding prenatal and postnatal care, and access to antibiotics for respiratory problems. Designing a comprehensive approach to even one of these factors with a limited population would consume the energy of even the most diligent and hard working medical missionary, yet with the right financial resources would be a relatively easy thing to do.

When I have evaluated what God's calling is for me and those I work with I keep coming back to the same thing—that cup of cold water. This translates into the following questions: *What basic needs are lacking here that I can work to provide which will positively affect the lives of the most people?* What is the cup of cold water that I need to prepare to give to these needy people given my own talents and resources which God has given me?

These are difficult questions and ones which are not easy to answer. We come from a land of plenty. Access to highly sophisticated and effective health care is widely available. So to change thinking patterns like this is difficult. In my US based clinic, 10% of the children I see there may have failure to thrive as a diagnosis for various reasons—the least of which is lack of access to food. In our clinic in Christ's Church of the City, nearly 90% of the children there exhibit moderate to severe malnutrition.

I would love to help the one or two blue babies I may see in a week long clinic there. But morally I am obligated to do what I can to change the situation for the 150 others who simply need more food. The blue baby most likely will die in Haiti. This is a hard fact to face but a true one. It is within my power to alter the futures of all those children who need more to eat or antibiotics for pneumonias to help them reach their fifth birthday.

I am not, in any way, advocating shunning or dehumanizing those we can't specifically help or those for whom we have no physical interventions. Quite the opposite. They need to be shown an extra measure of the compassion of the Christ we serve—as do their families. It is in these people that the real character of Christ will be manifest and we should be grateful for the opportunity to allow the Holy Spirit to work through us to them, as difficult as it may seem.

It borders on being immoral to use valuable financial, human and other resources to construct facilities or design programs which will provide services for a small select sub-group when such widespread basic needs exists within the population as a whole. I have seen this happen many times as good intentioned folks try to use the talent they have to help others.

My personal experience exemplifies this. Early in my work in Haiti, as I talked to the community leaders about what their perceived health care needs were, the first thing on their list was latrines. My initial response was—someone else who doesn't have my skills can do that—what else do you need? I can provide health care to you. What do you need for that?

However, as I thought about it, what I realized was that in this community of several thousand where no latrines existed, it seemed intuitive that having access to safe human waste disposal could only benefit them. Improper disposal of human waste exposes the population to diseases such as typhoid and intestinal parasites. Consequently, proper management of human waste in and of itself could improve the overall health of the community.

So I came home, pulled up everything I could find about latrines and latrine construction on the internet to educated myself. Given this was such a basic and critical need in the third world, there was no need to reinvent the wheel. The World Health Organization, among many others, had designed and implemented a program called Vision 21 which incorporated sanitation (latrines) and hygiene education. Thus, the genesis of our community wide sanitation project was conceived.

This was not rocket science, nor was it pediatric cardiology. But it was a fundamental need of the community which they perceived (and I agreed) would potentially bring a positive impact to a large number of people within the community—including the children. It was the only place to start.

I pursued getting funding and to date more than half the latrines have been built by the local people. The Haitians are in charge of the design and construction. We discussed their design which was good and with what I learned through my research, I suggested one design change which would increase the effectiveness and longevity of the latrine.

The next phase will be a community wide basic hygiene program. Data shows that simply disposing of human waste does not alone decrease the number of waste borne diseases in a population. It must be linked with a hygiene education program. This will be a home based hygiene program and will be based on the Medical Ambassadors community health educators program. Agent Sante's (community health workers) will be taught basic hygiene and then will bring the information to individuals households as well as evaluate it's effectiveness after a period of time.

We are involved in supporting the education of several medical students in Haiti. However, I believe that the community health worker approach will prove to be the most effective health care delivery system in Haiti given the current conditions and resources that they have available to them. When we evaluate how financial resources can be used to deliver the highest common denominator of health care to the masses, community health workers seem likely be the solution.

Basic needs such as prenatal evaluation and careful clean cutting of the umbilical cord have already altered the infant morbidity and mortality in many communities in a way that free standing clinics with regular missionaries and mission teams may not. These are simple and easy interventions which can be done economically. The potential impact on the target population will likely be significant.

No—this isn't curing cancer in Haiti, or fixing kids congenital heart defects. Nor is it even rehabilitating amputees. These are all worthy and noble efforts in the right circumstances. But in an environment where there is 80% unemployment, tenant farmers cannot grow anywhere near what they need to just feed their families, where the life expectancy is 49 years and 30% of the children die before age 5 from preventable causes, it is clear where the most work needs to be done.

So instead of the analogy of thinking big, I would encourage us to think smaller-think of the less sophisticated needs-the cup of cold water. Think about latrines instead of bone marrow transplants. Think about clean water instead of bypass surgery. Think about tetanus prevention in newborns instead of laparoscopic surgery facilities.

As you evaluate your talents and how you can use them to serve Him in your life, let God help you think out of the box. Look at all your talents—your basic high school education for one thing. I had never been trained in how to build a latrine. But my education and access to resources allowed me to learn-and very quickly at that.

For an entire year, each day I emptied my change into a jar I had sitting on the kitchen counter. I had set that money aside to use as scholarship money for one of our students we are supporting. Much to my surprise, at the end of the year when I counted it, there were several hundred dollars in it—literally disposable income for me. Money I easily did without but that meant support for nearly a whole year for a student in Haiti.

And when I want a chuckle at the sense of humor of our heavenly Father, I contrast my work weeks—one week I am involved in delivering and carrying out sophisticated procedures to alter the abnormal rhythms of a child's heart or teaching a mom how to care for her baby's new implanted pacemaker which will save him from a life threatening arrhythmia and sudden death. And the next week I am helping a small community construct out-houses and teaching them how to wash their hands and food utensils effectively to prevent spread of disease.

These work weeks are worlds apart—but my skills are equally needed in both worlds because God has placed me in each of them as an ambassador of His love. My job is only to be obedient and faithful to His calling. God has taught me much in my work in Haiti—humility and gratitude being the biggest things. And I have learned a measure of them in both of "my work worlds".

Yet despite my "cups of cold water" being so different in each of my worlds, what remains the same is the compassion that comes with service and through that the knowledge of the character of Christ that we grow into through it.

Now getting back to that cup of cold water, I am comforted when recalling this situation with the mothers in the waiting room. I cannot change poverty and disease in the world, Haiti, Nicaragua, the United States, North Carolina or even at Duke Hospital. I can't even help all the children I see here in the united States. But I can give 2 mothers in need a cup of ice. I can donate bottles of vitamins for malnourished children in Haiti. I can pray fervently and fast regularly for protection and strength, spiritual and physical, for the people ministering in Haiti and to those who suffer in faith there.

Each of these things may seem small and really without importance in this world that is so troubled, full of sin and without the grace and peace of the Lord Jesus Christ. It is overwhelming for me to try to imagine what my small contribution of medical and nursing skills or even skills in building an outhouse, can do to solve these problems. Indeed, my contributions won't solve these problems.

But I can make a difference for one person at one moment on one day of his or her life.

The Father has called us to one thing—to be faithful and obedient to Him. That is what those who minister to the poor in Haiti, in Sudan, in Honduras, and in inner city Chicago are trying to do—and they are doing it quite effectively in circumstances many of us in the developed world would find hard to even imagine.

He changes things.

He soothes the troubled heart and forgives sin.

He heals the sick.

He comforts the grief stricken and those that are mourning

He gives riches above all expectation.

We need only be the willing vessel who prays or gives the one cup of ice or one bottle of vitamins or helps build the one latrine that makes the difference for that person at that moment.

The renowned gospel hymn writer put it simply yet so profoundly when he wrote:

"If just a cup of water I place within your hand,
then just a cup of water is all that I demand."[2]

CHAPTER NINE

Little is much in Balais, Haiti

"'All we have are five loaves of bread and two fish," they said.
Jesus said, "Bring them here."
Then he had the people sit on the grass. He took the five loaves
and two fish, lifted his face to heaven in prayer, blessed, broke, and
gave the bread to the disciples. The disciples then gave the food to
the congregation. They all ate their fill. They gathered twelve
baskets of leftovers. About five thousand were fed.
Matt. 14: 19-20 (The Message)

The day started early. We left at 6AM although we probably should have left earlier. The ride to Balais was long—3 1/2 hours over fairly good roads for Haiti. It was a part of the country I had not seen before and instead of a lush tropical island, I felt more like we were in the deserts of Africa. The terrain was flat, arid, cactus laden, and except for the ocean that we drove beside for about 20 miles, there was no sign of water.

About a month before our trip, I had been asked to visit a small village in a remote area of Haiti that had a group of believers who were worshipping under the pastoral leadership of my friend, the local pastor. He had graduated from Bible College in Haiti 2 years ago. He had heard of this church through a friend. They were a small group of Christians, about 100, whose pastor had left.

Pastor Charles visited Balais and felt called to go there to preach. He makes the rough 6 hour tap tap ride-Haitian public transportation-on Saturday and returns on Tuesday. He preaches on Saturday night, 2 times on Sunday and Monday night before returning. They are trying to start a small school and he thought we might be able to help them with some school supplies.

I agreed to visit. Prior to going to Haiti, I had purchased all of the school supplies we could fit into a backpack. With some creative packing, it turned out to be quite a bit.

I was also told they needed a blackboard. So before we left Port au Prince, I was able to buy 2- 4 x 4 blackboards for $3 US. I grabbed my water bottle, and stuck some toilet paper in my backpack. I had learned from my few days in the city already that there are no public rest rooms for a woman to use the bathroom. Since we were going into the wilderness, I thought the options would be few and wanted to be prepared.

So our journey began. I was grateful for the ride. I take advantage of any time I can get with my Haitian friends. So 7 hours in a car was wonderful for me. I got to know Pastor Charles much better as we made the trek. He is a sweet man with a gentle spirit of the Lord. He has 4 children and lives in a small 3 room house in Port au Prince that I also visited when we picked him up. His faith, like most of the Haitian Christians I have met, is one to be admired and emulated.

About 30 minutes from our destination, my friend Remy, who also helps Pastor Charles preach there once a month, turned to me and said "You know the whole village will be waiting for you".

Well, I didn't know that. It was at this point I realized this was not going to be just an ordinary day.

We got to the place where we needed to park, and began the one mile hike to the river we would need to cross. I had seen pictures of the hollowed out tree canoe that would take us to Balais across a raging rapid river. I was looking forward to that part but had no idea of what was also waiting for me on the other bank of the river. I caught sight of the myriad of colors on the opposite bank about 100 yards before we reached the canoe.

There were about 100 people standing there with an umbrella or two to shade them from the sun. My heart started to flutter at this sight as I began to realize just what was going to happen. The whole village had gathered to meet me. I began to hear sounds from that direction which would become clearer as we got closer. They were singing a wonderful Kreyol song of welcome. They had waited about an hour for the American missionary to come visit.

We made our way down the steep bank to the canoe dock, loaded everything, including the blackboards, into the canoe and began the ride across the river that was about 400 yards wide. Our canoe "driver" was experienced and got us across easily in about 15 minutes. We couldn't even get out of the canoe before the people, continuing their singing, rushed down the bank, unloaded and carried everything we had brought.

The people, adults and children, literally surrounded me, grabbed my hands, clothing and anything else they could hold onto and escorted me up the hill. We walked about another mile to the church. They continued to sing the entire time. The harmonies that came out of this beautiful choir that surrounded me are hard to describe. I was overwhelmed but trying desperately to take in everything too. I asked Remy what they were singing and he told me it was a Haitian praise song thanking God for keeping them in their lives. They also sang another Haitian song of greeting.

As we made our way to the church whose walls were made of banana leaves and a thatched roof, I realized that this was truly a once in a lifetime experience. The whole village gathered in the small 20 x 20 hut they used as a church. Half of the people there were children and they were all in the front. There were 2 wooden chairs in the front of the church designated for us. Remy and I took our assigned places.

The community leaders brought me greetings that Remy translated for me and then Remy told me I could speak to them. When I asked if I could stand up he told me that I should stay seated, out of respect to them offering me the only chairs there. Using Remy as my translator, I greeted them in the name of our Lord and talked to them about my visit. The children had prepared a song and sang it to me. The Kreyol translation is "Welcome visitor to our village today. We are glad you have come. Welcome visitor today."

We went to one of the community leader's home where I was told they had prepared food for us. The whole house was smaller than my own bedroom at home and had 2 very small rooms, one with a small bed and the other with 3 wooden chairs and a small table. This is the bed that Pastor Charles and Remy sleep in when they come to preach. The owners sleep outside on the ground so the pastors can have a bed.

All of the village people remained outside while we ate. Most of them would not eat that day themselves, yet they waited while we ate, as did our hosts. It was a simple lunch-beans, rice and cooked chicken. However, in this community where meat is scarce, I knew sacrifices had been made to prepare it. While I realize there is a risk of sickness in eating food prepared by the Haitians, I also know that it is prepared usually with some degree of sacrifice and as a gift offering for guests. I prayed for the food and ate. In these situations where I feel compelled to do things that might be risky, I find that I must trust our Lord to keep me safe especially in situations like this where I know the food is literally a gift. I would want to do nothing to offend my Haitian brothers and sisters.

It is a deeply humbling experience to know that someone has sacrificed so you can eat when they are not eating themselves. However, when the water was passed, Remy did tell me I should not drink it. So I politely declined.

After eating we went out and talked more to the people. As I held children on my lap, Remy began talking to them. Because I knew some Kreyol, after a minute or two I figured out what he was saying. He was telling them of my illness after coming to Haiti in October and as a result, the risk that I take each time I return to Haiti because of the Dengue Fever.

Just 8 months before I had gone to Haiti with a group shortly after 9/11. It was in October, the height of the rainy season and while the weather was hot, there seemed to be more mosquitoes than I remembered before. There were several places where water was standing daily in the clinic due to torrential rains the night before. These pools of water serve as breeding grounds for mosquitoes.

I had taken insect repellant spray with me and did spray pretty regularly during the week. But at the end of the week I noticed that there were quite a few bites on my lower leg, between the area where my sock ended and my dress hem began. I gave no real further thought to them except when they itched.

We returned home on a Sunday and I went to work as planned on Monday. I had lunch with a friend who works in Haiti also, sharing my experiences of that trip. I felt fine as we ate and shared the stories of my trip. However when I returned to my office only minutes later, I began to feel quite ill very suddenly. I noted that my body ached all over and I began to shiver violently at my desk. I went into an exam room in our clinic and took my temperature. It was 104 degrees.

I knew I was in trouble and immediately contacted one of the physicians I work with whose husband is board certified in tropical medicine. I asked her if I could call him because I was sure I had malaria or dengue fever.

He told me to go immediately to the Emergency Room of our medical center and called there to give them a heads up on my coming. Within the hour, I was violently ill. The aches were nearly unbearable; I was having shaking chills from the high fever and could barely make it to the ER without assistance.

A spinal tap, CAT scan of my head, blood cultures and other lab work ruled out the more common things that patients presenting with these symptoms in our medical center might have like meningitis, flu etc. Given the sudden onset of the symptoms, my history of multiple mosquito bites, my recent return from Haiti where Dengue Fever is endemic, it became clear, that it was likely Dengue Fever.

I was admitted to the hospital and gratefully so. I didn't argue with the physician assistant when she said I needed to be admitted. I felt so awful the thought of trying to take care of myself was unthinkable at that moment.

Dengue Fever is a viral infection which is spread by mosquitoes. The mosquito infects the person when they bite them. It is also known as "break bone fever" because of the severe shaking chills which one has in response to the fevers. I can attest that the shivering is so violent that it does feel like your bones would break.

I remained hospitalized for 7 days. The first 5 days I was very ill and not very aware of what was going on around me. Because it is a viral illness, there is no real treatment except supportive measures to help the person survive until their body can fight off and contain the virus. These measures include medications to help control the fevers and intravenous fluids. In addition, the virus attacks the blood cells, specifically the white blood cells which fight off infections and the platelets, the cells necessary to form clots. My blood counts were very low. My white count was less than 1000 (normal being 3000-10,000) and my platelet counts were less than 20,000 (normal being 150,000-450,000). When this happens, platelet transfusions are needed to prevent spontaneous hemorrhaging.

The problem with these kinds of blood counts is that a person is now susceptible to other infections that their body otherwise might fight off on its own. They are also at high risk of bleeding because of the low cells that make blood clots to form to stop bleeding. When this complication occurs, it is known as Hemorrhagic Dengue Fever. This happens in about 30% of the people who get Dengue Fever.

About 5 days after the fevers, the illness is characterized by a bright red rash usually on the extremities. Mine came later but it came with a vengeance. Both of my calves were bright red with a generalized rash.

I was discharged after 7 days to go home to recuperate. The fevers had abated by then and I felt I would do better at home. It took another full two weeks before I felt like going back to work. The fatigue continued for nearly two months before I felt like I was back to normal. Three other people on my team got less intense forms of Dengue Fever that week. None required hospitalization but all were quite ill.

I clearly remember one night when the fevers were very bad. I began praying that God would take me home to be with Him. I would have welcomed death over how I was feeling then.

I also remember one coherent time when I thought how grateful I was that I was here in this medical center being cared for by people who had my well being first in their minds in the comfort of this facility and that I was not lying in one of those shanties in Haiti in the urban slum where we worked trying to recover there. Later when I reflected on that thought, it truly made me empathize with the degree of suffering that happens there every moment of every day in Haiti.

My Dengue Fever was documented by the results of my blood tests about 4 weeks later. These are not typically run at major medical centers and need to be sent off to the CDC. It did document the type that I had and unfortunately because to the type I had and the fact that my platelet count got so low, it makes me a very high risk for developing the hemorrhagic form of the disease if I were to get it again.

The importance of this is that, because of the high risk of getting hemorrhagic type which is often fatal, my doctor strongly recommended that I not return to Haiti. When he told me that, my heart sank. I couldn't believe that God would give me this very redeeming experience and then take it right away. Over the next few months I fervently prayed and had many prayer warriors pray with me about returning to Haiti. After seeking Him, I felt confident that I was to return and put my future in His hands.

This trip to Balais was my first trip to Haiti since being ill. As I realized that this was the story that Remy was telling, I insisted that he let me tell more of the story. I told them of my love for the Haitian people, the precious gifts of themselves they had given me and my strong desire to return to Haiti. I spoke of the assurance that I had from our Father that He would protect me as long as I was in His will and of my hope that this would minister to my doctors and those who questioned my choice to return. They clapped and cheered. I ended with prayers for them. The Lord's spirit was clearly in the midst of us.

I met some more with the leaders, distributed our school supplies and then talked with Pastor Charles about what he saw the needs to be. I saw the 5 acres that he had purchased with his own money to eventually build a church for his people. This community of subsistence farmers has no latrines, or tested clean water source. Most of the children are malnourished. They have no access to medical care or a school. The only semblance of one is a small one room class which meets sporadically when someone who knows how to read and write can get to them. It is a community of great needs.

As we left, my heart was jubilant but also very heavy. A community with so little, yet so much.

This is the story of Haiti. These are people of tremendous faith. They love and worship God with a fervor I have seen rarely in our own country. We didn't talk as much on the way home. My mind was racing trying to process what had just happened to me.

Yes, the canoe ride was exciting. But in contrast to everything else, it is greatly overshadowed by the people of Balais. I had experienced again, as I have too many times to count, the graciousness and generosity of people who have nothing, and yet who offer what they have to others. I had experienced strength of Christian faith in people whose material possessions are very little. I doubt that my own faith would ever be that strong. I also experienced Pastor Charles and Remy's commitment to this small but faithful group of believers. God was just beginning to make clear to me what I was to do with this experience.

For some time now I have felt that my calling for Haiti is not to help "the people of Haiti" but to help "people of Haiti". As I have invested time to develop and foster relationships with individuals, God has drawn me closer to Him through His beloved children of Haiti.

Thursday May 2, 2002 is a day that will be forever etched in my memory. I will always be extremely grateful to Pastor Charles and Remy for providing me with this experience that has literally changed my life. It has humbled me in a way nothing else could.

God is at work in Haiti. Stories like this are not rare there. There are many that are sacrificing greatly under the direst of circumstances to see that the Lord's work is advanced there. Pray that we will be as faithful here in the places where we live and work as are our brothers and sisters of Haiti.

CHAPTER TEN

But God, *every* need

"You can be sure that God will take care of everything
you need..."
Philippians 4:19 (The Message)

It is not completely unprecedented to discuss bathrooms in a public forum. I recall one of our local missionaries telling us at her last visit to our church in our Sunday morning service of over-hearing a conversation while she was stationed in a bathroom stall. Another young missionary recently shared with us the experience of witnessing to a person in a bathroom at her wedding.

So while it may not be the usual topic of discussions on missions, it isn't the first time it has come up either. One finds out quickly when one does mission work that the seemingly simplest things we take for granted here in the US become pretty significant things when working for the Lord in a developing world country. And bathroom facilities are one of those things. This story illustrates this concept.

I was invited to visit a remote village in rural Haiti by a pastor of a small village Christian church. The pastor has been ministering in the community of Balais for about 2 years. He travels 2.5 hours each week to the village by Haitian tap-tap (the Haitian version of public transportation-it may be a large bus or a converted pick up truck). Each Thursday he begins his journey there and stays until Monday, holding services each evening. The church is made of banana leaf walls, the pews are made of slices of local trees that are about 6 inches wide-not really very "bottom friendly". Over 100 faithful Christians worship each week with him.

I had visited this community for one day last summer and was completely taken by the sincerity of the people and the strength of their Christian faith in the most difficult of circumstances. The people there are very poor. All are subsistence farmers. No one has a job outside the community.

At this humble pastor's invitation, I had decided to do a pediatric clinic for two days to evaluate the general health of the children in this community for future intervention and to treat any problems that I could. I would need to ride 3 hours on rough roads (only about 35 miles but the roads were so bad it would take that long), hike about a mile across a prairies like area, cross a river in a hollowed out canoe and then hike about 2 more miles to reach the village. I could only take with me what I could carry over that distance.

However, I knew there was going to be a problem. One of the things that the community lacked resources to build was latrines. The people were just too poor to use their meager incomes to build latrines or outhouses. Most of them only made about $100 per year. It presented a problem to us, one our hosts were very concerned about as well. I was the first missionary to come to this village and they were very conscious of the lack of sanitation facilities for me.

I decided to plan to go and to deal with it as best I could. Beginning about 2 months before the trip, each week I dedicated time to plan, pray and fast for the trip. There are no hotels or guest-houses nearby so I had been invited to stay in the home of a Haitian family for the duration.

Now, I am not an expert camper or have I had a lot of experi-ence with this kind of situation. Prior to this experience, my idea of roughing it was a Motel 6® instead of a Holiday Inn ®. But I had a lot of support.

My sister made me a bag of the necessary things-a small shovel, toilet paper, hand sanitizer, bug spray, etc. to make do in the woods as the people in Balais did each day. However, I was more than a little anxious at the thought of nearly 4 days without a semblance of a bathroom as I knew it. Maybe one day would have been manageable, but 4 days were nerve wracking at the very least.

The day arrived for me to leave the guesthouse in Port au Prince for our adventure. My anxiety was not allayed very much by the prayer I had with my Haitian companions before we left. I was going to be living in a home in the village of one of the community leaders, Monsieur Occident. We arrived at the river bank, donned our backpacks, loaded ourselves up with our supplies in our duffels and, with my 3 Haitian companions, headed off across the river. What a sight it must have been. When we arrived at the house we were to stay in, we had a wonderful welcoming of the village people who were there to greet us with songs and hugs of welcome.

The house we were to stay in was a typical Haitian home- comprised of two small rooms of about 8 x 8 '. One was a bedroom, the other a living room with a single bed in it. The floors were dirt, the walls plaster and stucco and the frame typical Haitian wood.

Our hosts showed me to their bedroom, which they graciously gave up for me while I was there. The room contained a double bed and small table. They had prepared for me by having clean linens on the bed and mosquito netting over the bed to protect me from mosquitoes and the diseases they carry. They had placed a fuel lantern on the table for me to use as a light source in the evenings.

Well, I was here and still quite nervous but at least I had made it this far. My dear friend and companion Remy finally broached the subject we had been avoiding and asked us if I would like to see where we would use the bathroom. Taking a deep breath and straightening my pretty non existent backbone, I said OK. I followed him out the back door and into the corn field.

"OK, I can do this", I just kept saying over in my mind.

About 20 feet into the corn field, I saw a small slab of concrete with a few pieces of tin roofing balancing on it in makeshift walls. I didn't remember seeing this on my trip there a few months before.

As we rounded this structure, Remy stated, "Here is your latrine."

In front of me was a sight for sore eyes. A concrete slab was there with a cement commode on top of it. Corrugated tin walls surrounded the latrine for privacy. In my amazement, all I could say was "Where did this come from".

"We built it for you", Remy answered "because we knew you were coming."

Now an outhouse like what I was looking at might have looked pretty horrible had you just seen it alone. But it was a wonderful gift for me and a sight for sore eyes to a scared, apprehensive American missionary nervous about doing without a bathroom, as I knew one.

To say I was shocked would have been an understatement. But once my shock wore off, I realized what had really happened here. Sacrifices, really significant ones, had been made for me to have a convenience I was used to. These weren't the last sacrifices I was to see people make for me in Haiti. I was later to find out that this latrine had cost about $50 US to build, nearly half of our hosts annual income.

When I realized this, I was completely overcome with humility—people who didn't even know me would sacrifice food for their family to build a latrine for me simply because I took the time to show them with my presence that I cared.

As the events of the week unfolded, I was more than a little grateful for that cement potty. When my companion became quite ill and was lying on a straw mat on the outskirts of a corn field, it was these same blessed, gracious people who surrounded her feverish body with constant prayers. These same people graciously gave to us what they had, even though it was too little for even them. God showed me that week that I cannot make it on my own strength. More than anything, I realized that I need Him to sustain me. It took that cement potty to represent that and the great sacrifices of my host to me. God does truly meet *every* need and nothing is too small for Him to provide for us.

Gratitude is the thing that I have found most since beginning working in Haiti—gratitude for the many rich blessings we have here. But also for the wondrous joy of coming to know the gracious people of Haiti.

CHAPTER ELEVEN

Lord, Teach Me to Pray

"One day Jesus was praying in a certain place.
When he finished, one of his disciples said to him,
"Lord, teach us to pray...."
Luke 11:1 (NLT)

It is true that I pray a lot when I am in Haiti.

My friend once said to someone in front of me, "Most people stop their lives to pray; April stops praying to live."

I wish that were really true. But I do find myself praying a lot in Haiti, for a couple of reasons. First, my own personal safety is never far from my mind. In a country where there is a degree of political unrest, my own knowledge of any particular culture situation is far from adequate, I can only communicate with stuttered and basic Kreyol and where I am clearly in the minority with regards to socioeconomic status, race and ethnicity, I am very concerned about others response to me.

But more than that, I am much more AWARE of my need for God in Haiti. The truth is that I need God all the time, but I am aware of that need in an acute way in Haiti—much more so than here in the states. When doing mission work in Haiti, one must leave ones independence at the door to the airplane. We find ourselves nearly completely dependant on our hosts for most of the things we handle ourselves while living our lives in the states. Thus my need for strength outside of my own is always present leading to my awareness of my need for the strength of the Father. Things I could handle easily here, I need to rely on others or strength outside of my own for in Haiti.

The first day of one of our trips to Balais, Haiti was no different. We were a small medical team, doing a pediatric clinic in a remote village in Haiti where we had been invited. Our team had been assembled partly by me here in the US and partly by Remy, my Haitian friend. My American companion and I were to be traveling with Remy and Justus as translators and Philippe who would be our driver and help us in the clinic with paperwork. They would serve as our companions, living and working together in a remote village in Haiti, residing with a family of the village and staying in close quarters for 4 days.

Before we left we gathered as a team together in the guest house conference room for a time of meditation and prayer together. We were leaving later than we anticipated but this was important. I had asked the Lord what His message would be to me and this group. We knew Remy but didn't know Justus or Philippe, our driver and additional translator or they, us.

As I prayed, I felt led to share with them 2 passages, John 15: 1-9:

"I am the true vine, and my Father is the gardener. He cuts off every branch in me that bears no fruit, while every branch that does bear fruit he prunes so that it will be even more fruitful. You are already clean because of the word I have spoken to you. Remain in me, and I will remain in you. No branch can bear fruit by itself; it must remain in the vine. Neither can you bear fruit unless you remain in me. I am the vine; you are the branches. If a man remains in me and I in him, he will bear much fruit; apart from me you can do nothing. If anyone does not remain in me, he is like a branch that is thrown away and withers; such branches are picked up, thrown into the fire and burned. If you remain in me and my words remain in you, ask whatever you wish, and it will be given you. This is to my Father's glory, that

*you bear much fruit, showing yourselves to be my disciples.
As the Father has loved me, so have I loved you. Now
remain in my love." (NIV)*

I wanted to make the point that our strength ultimately comes
only from God. Related to this passage, I read 1 Corinthians
12:14-21:

*"Now the body is not made up of one part but of many. If the
foot should say, 'Because I am not a hand, I do not belong to
the body,' it would not for that reason cease to be part of the
body. And if the ear should say, 'Because I am not an eye, I
do not belong to the body,' it would not for that reason cease
to be part of the body. If the whole body were an eye, where
would the sense of hearing be? If the whole body were an
ear, where would the sense of smell be? But in fact God has
arranged the parts in the body, every one of them, just as he
wanted them to be. If they were all one part, where would the
body be? As it is, there are many parts, but one body. The eye
cannot say to the hand, 'I don't need you!' And the head
cannot say to the feet, 'I don't need you!" (NIV)*

Here Paul clearly entreats us to realize our interdependence by
describing the parts of the body. Where would the eyes be without
the ears, and the ears without the hands? Each is important in
getting the task done. We were a team-being the body of Christ to
the people we were to minister to. If we were to be successful at the
task at hand, we needed to realize within ourselves that we all
needed each other.

We had a special time of prayer together. This has become a
tradition for me with all the teams I travel with and lead. We formed
a circle and each of us prayed for the person to our left, bringing
them specifically before the Father asking for strength and knowledge to carry out His work. Our friends prayed in Kreyol and we
prayed in English. I concluded with a prayer for us as a group.

We were going out to literally be the body of Christ. "Eyes,
ears, hands..." that is a phrase which was spoken often as a task

would come up which required all of us to pull together to accomplish. The Haitian's are so gracious-they would literally do everything if we would let them. We had much to carry and a long way to carry it once we arrived. Yet we would say-"Remember, eyes, ears, and hands...", and they would allow us to do our share. We were truly the body of Christ in a way I have never been before-a small yet able group through the power of the Holy Spirit.

As I readied for bed that first night, I was filled with a great deal of anxiety at the thought of sleeping in a strange bed in a house with dirt floors and a latrine to use (although you already know what a great blessing the latrine was for me especially when I considered the alternative). The story of the spider on the wall of our bedroom is one unto itself, but it doesn't take much to see in your mind's eye the comical mental image of two young American women in the countryside of Haiti, clutching each other outside the house as we called to our able friend, Remy, to assess the situation and rid our room of a giant spider on the wall. He assured us it was not a tarantula and that he had indeed killed it (although we never saw the carcass) but it was still very frightening. Remy left our room by telling us to please call him at anytime in the night time that we needed anything. Regardless of his attempts at reassurance, when we finally got under our mosquito netting, we weren't any less anxious.

Yet, I was filled with a deep sense of peace as the events of the next few minutes unfolded. Our 5 Christian brothers had taken their places, lying, side by side, on a straw palate on the dirt floor in the room right next to us. As I tried to quiet my heart and mind for sleep, I heard them break out in spontaneous and concerted prayers out loud.

They made no effort to do this quietly. They were all praying in Kreyol, simultaneously, out loud and together.

I was awestruck.

It was as if it was just apart of the bedtime ritual for them-which it clearly was. I have heard Haitians pray this way in church and it is a wonder to behold. But as I lay in my bed that dark night in rural Haiti, with the only light available the few stars overhead and the only other sounds the crickets and frogs, I was overcome with the majesty of the presence of the Holy Spirit as our friends prayed before going off to sleep.

Because I know and can understand and speak some Kreyol, it was clear that they were praying for *us*. "Sere Avril" (Sister April) were words which were clearly audible and heard often, even in a foreign language. The cacophony was beautiful and soothing. They ended one at a time and after about 15 minutes each voice faded out, leaving one less until the last one finished.

Funny, I had not even thought to pray during my fright. But their example is one that again shows me the depth of their faith, their lack of self consciousness in expressing it and thus their close communion with our Father.

That was not the last we were to hear of our Haitian brothers in Christ prayers that night. It was about 3:30 AM and I was startled awake by what seemed to be very loud singing directly outside the door to my room. As I listened, I heard our host, the owner of the home we were staying in, begin his singing and praying time-the Haitian version of his "quiet time". At first it was unnerving-being so early in the morning and also startling.

People in Haiti are so used to living in very close quarters. It is not unusual for 10-12 people to occupy two rooms with only one bed. Sleeping is often done in shifts and turns are taken for sleeping in the bed. As one can see, in situations like this, concerns with the possibility of disturbing others becomes pointless and thus an exercise in futility—understandably so.

But as I listened to his songs and prayers to the Lord, I realized that this man LIVED his faith. He was up long before dawn, spending the time with the Lord that one needs in order to stay in close communion with him, praying for the missionaries who were staying with him.

I clearly heard our names in his prayers also. How humbling that they would bring us to the Father in this way.

I am trying to achieve what Paul teaches us when he instructs us to be in a constant state of prayer. Little did I realize that I would come to rely completely on God through prayer in a way I never have before in my life in less that 48 hours time.

CHAPTER TWELVE

The Hem of His Garment

"For she thought, "If I just touch His garments, I will get well."
Mark 5:28 (NIV)

I had traveled to Balais with a friend of mine, Susan. She had
served as our pharmacist in the clinic while I saw patients. It
was a joy to travel with her. We had scheduled a focus group meeting with a group of women after our last day of clinic. We were to
meet with them at 6 PM at the church.

Our time with them took about an hour. After that, the church
was having a special service in our honor. We were tired but wanted
to honor their gift to us. It was about 9 PM when the service ended.

We were all sitting together outside the house we were staying
in. I was trying to translate some of the praise songs that we sing in
our church into Kreyol with our friends. I had hoped to teach them
to our congregation at home.

Susan looked over at me and said, "I don't feel too well. I think
I am going to bed."

I knew when I looked at her that she wasn't well. She walked
towards the back of the house. I thought maybe I should go with
her. As I followed her to the back of the house, she began vomiting.

We went inside the house to the bedroom. She was feeling quite
ill. I took her temperature and it was 104. I knew she was sick.

When I travel to Haiti, I try to be as prepared as I can be for medical situations such as these. We often find ourselves in places where we cannot get medical care. For that reason we need to be self sufficient. I have set up a mini hospital at our guest house where we have had IV's running and antibiotics being given for team members that have succumbed to the illnesses common in Haiti.

I began immediately to treat the fever. I gave her Tylenol and something to help with the nausea. I wanted to start an IV but she was afraid of that and agreed she would try to drink if it would mean she wouldn't get an IV. So I agreed for the time being.

We made a drink out of Gatorade powder that I carried with us. I told her how much she had to drink and in what period of time. She said she would do her best.

I told my Haitian companions that my friend was ill and I needed their help to tend to her. By this time the vomiting had started again and quite violently. She also began to have diarrhea. I was very concerned for her fluid status given she was loosing fluids both through vomiting and diarrhea.

I approached the IV idea again, but she said she would drink. Thinking she might have dysentery commonly seen in these kinds of situations, I started her on Cipro, a strong antibiotic. Throughout the night, we woke her hourly to make her drink. I was able to control the vomiting with compazine. But despite the medication, she still had a fever.

The Haitians were very concerned about her. They did everything they could to help me. They supplied me with water to cool her skin trying to break the fever. When she was nauseous, they helped with that. One time during the night, I woke up to find one of our translators standing by her bed praying that God would heal her.

The next morning was the morning we were scheduled to leave. It was clear we couldn't. My friend was still ill and feverish. So early in the morning, I sent one of the Haitians to travel the three hours back to Port au Prince to tell our other Haitian host we would be late returning to the city. They were expecting us back on that day and I didn't want to create excessive worry over nothing. I expected we would leave the next day.

Susan's fever was still high at 101 despite Tylenol and Cipro. Now 12 hours after the first Cipro, I had hoped that her fever might be better but it wasn't. She was able to drink so I delayed putting in an IV.

However, controlling the fever was going to be needed. She had been lying in the hot house with little ventilation. I wondered if we could try to move her outside sometime just so she might not be so hot. I mentioned this idea to Remy to see what he thought. I heard him go out and speak to some of the other Haitians but didn't pay much more attention to it.

In a few minutes, Remy returned to tell me that had arranged a place outside for my friend. I walked outside to see what he was referring to. Under a small tree about 20 feet from the house was a small clearing. Around this clearing, the people had put up three "walls" of woven banana leaves making a small sick room outside. This would allow ventilation yet still block out the sun. There was a straw pallet lying on the ground for her to lie on. It was amazing how resourceful they had been with what little they had. They had made the "sick room".

I went back into the bedroom and said, "Susan, we are going to move you outside. I think you will be more comfortable out there."

She agreed and moved slowly outside to the pallet. She laid down and almost immediately she was asleep. I decided rest and fluids would help break the fever so we let her rest for several hours without waking her. We cooled her skin with sponge baths to try to bring the fever down.

At this time, I began to feel worried. Her fever was still high. She had had two doses of Cipro. That and Tylenol were not bringing the fever down like I wanted. As long as her temp was over 101, I was worried. When she didn't take the compazine, she would vomit. She continued to drink adequately though so I help off on the IV at her insistence.

During the afternoon, our Haitian companions, including Remy pulled their chairs around her and would sing quietly and pray for her. It was a sweet scene to see. They asked me to try to rest while they tended to her knowing I had been up most of the night with her.

That evening, I decided I had held off on the IV long enough. In addition, I felt the Cipro probably wasn't what we needed. We also carried Rocephin with us. It is a strong antibiotic that needs to be given through a shot. I told Susan I needed to give her some Rocephin. She was very familiar with the routine as she had given it several times during our clinic to sick children.

It was about 7 PM when I gave the injection. I decided I would wait 12 hours to see how it would work. Right at that time, Pastor Charles who had gone to Port au Prince to deliver the message, returned saying he had made contact with our other Haitian host. They were glad I had sent him and would expect us the next day.

I was exhausted-emotionally and physically. I needed rest to be able to think clearer. So I went to bed. I asked Remy to wake me in two hours to take Susan's temperature. When he did, he told me he had already taken it. It was 102 still.

I began to really worry now. Her temperature wasn't going down. I had done everything I knew to do and had used all the resources I had available to me. We needed to leave tomorrow. I had been praying all day that God would heal Susan. It just wasn't happening. My biggest concern was that she clearly couldn't travel in this condition. She could hardly make it to the latrine.

I sat there on the small bed in the room which served as living room, kitchen and bedroom of this small house. It was at this time that I realized I was really scared. I didn't know what else to do. I was there alone with no one to consult with having to make all the important decisions myself. We were three hours from the city and no way to get us home. Susan couldn't travel in the condition she was in.

I put my head in my hands and I began praying, out loud, without inhibition, much like the prayers of the Haitians I have described before. I have never prayed quite like this before. I have cried out to God but never in front of others. It was clear my own strength would not work here. I had to rely on God and I needed His help to do that.

I still had my head in my hands when I finished praying. Remy was sitting beside me.

Quietly he put his hand on my shoulder and said, "April, God will make a way for us. We just have to trust Him."

I knew Remy was right. I had a peace in my heart and decided I needed to make good use of my time. I needed to rest because I didn't know what tomorrow would hold for us. We had to get back to the city. I didn't know how God would do it but I knew He would get us back.

I told everyone I was going to bed. I asked them to wake me at 5 AM so I could see how Susan was and then decide what we should do.

Exhaustion took over and I slept for 5 hours. My Haitian friends got up each hour during the night to check on Susan. I was grateful for their help.

When 5 AM came it wasn't quite light yet. I needed to use the flash light to put in my contact lenses. Remy was up and sitting outside.

When I came out, I asked him "How are we going to get Susan to the truck. She cannot walk that far and we need to get back to Port au Prince?'

"I am not sure, yet. Let's just pray some more" he replied.

So I went back in to check on Susan. Her temperature was 99.9. I was relieved but she was still very weak. She couldn't really drink much but at least her vomiting and diarrhea had stopped. She asked me what we were going to do. I told her I wasn't sure yet.

I went back outside.

Remy came up to me and asked "Can she ride a horse?"

"I think so. Do we have one?" I asked.

"Yes, we have a small horse. If she can ride that to the river, I think we can make it to the truck."

"Please, let's try that." I agreed.

In about 5 minutes, I saw our host leading a small horse that he had borrowed from a neighbor through the field. The pony had a small Haitian blanket and saddle on it. I was sure this would work. I knew this was God's solution. I felt like Abraham when he saw the ram in the thicket. This was our answer. God had provided.

I went in and told Susan what we were going to do. She had never ridden a horse before but felt she could hang on enough to get to the river.

What a parade we made. Many people from the community came to help us leave. They carried all of our equipment and bags we had brought for the clinic. In addition I asked that we take a chair so if Susan got tired, she could sit down. Our hosts' son carried the chair right beside Susan as she rode the horse.

When we got to the river, we unloaded Susan from the horse and let her rest in the chair for a while. In the meantime, we loaded all of the bags and equipment into the canoe and sent it over to the other side of the river. People were waiting on the other side to help us carry it to the truck.

When all of that was over, we loaded Susan, me, Remy, our host's son and the chair in the last canoe and started over. What a comical picture that was. The chair in the canoe-can you imagine.

When we got to the other side, we put Susan in the chair once again and let her rest. We only had about 1/2 mile to go to the truck. She felt with rest and time, she could make it. So we traveled slowly, letting her sit down in the chair on the footpath when she was tired.

I had asked Pastor Charles if he would go ahead and load the truck with the bags and equipment. He graciously did. I also gave him a blanket and pillow and asked him to make a small area in the truck for Susan to lie down in when she got there. It took us about an hour to make it that half mile to the truck. Susan made it but was exhausted.

We situated her in the makeshift bed, said a quick good bye to our friends and started on the road back to the city. I asked Susan to try to drink something before we left. She complied but then immediately fell asleep before we even left.

We made the three hour trip back to Port au Prince without event. We tucked Susan into bed at the guest house. We were grateful that the one room which had air conditioning was available so we took it. I immediately phoned my friend who was a board certified Infectious Disease physician in the states. I wanted to know if there was anything else I should do. We had tried to get a commercial flight out early but there was nothing for two days until our own booked flights left. Given that Susan's fever was gone, she felt a little better although still ill, it was hard to justify a med-evac. He said just to continue the Cipro and keep her well hydrated. When she got home she needed to see someone immediately.

We arrived home safe and sound a couple of days later. Susan went to her physician. He ran blood tests and found she had acute pancreatitis. He felt the cause was likely something in the food she had eaten. He was relieved we had the medication and IV supplies we had to support her until we could get home. It took her two weeks to fully recover.

I heard someone say once that when you've slipped and reached rope's end, it is there you will find the hem of His garment.[6] That night in Balais, I had reached my rope's end. I had done everything I could. I had used all my resources.

It was then that I found the hem of His garment. When Remy reminded me that God had promised to make a way for us, like the woman with the bleeding in the Bible, I felt I had touched the hem of His garment. If my faith could just believe that He would make a way, it would be so. And He did make a way—on the back of a horse.

I guess what my friend said might be more right now than it was before. Yes, I pray a lot in Haiti. But I pray a lot more here at home too.

CHAPTER THIRTEEN

Voodoo-a wolf in sheep's clothing

"For such people are not serving our Lord Christ,
but their own appetites. By smooth talk and flattery they deceive
the minds of naive people."
Romans 16:18 (NIV)

The first image that many people have about Haiti is one of voodoo. The mental image of voodoo that they have is one which has been born of the Hollywood films —a witchdoctor or other voodoo practitioner using pins in a voodoo doll to inflict harm on another at the request of their customer. Or perhaps they think immediately of the mummified zombie, rising from the grave to walk among the living terrorizing them.

I wish that were all voodoo was because those myths could easily be dispelled and we would be rid of the influence of voodoo in Haiti culture. Voodoo like any other animistic belief system, is based in the world of the spirits. Sprits are both ancestrally based and celestially based (spirits that God himself has created). Animism is a belief that the unseen spirits act daily in the lives of people, both for good and bad. These spirits represent God but are not necessarily controlled by Him or work at His command. While God is still seen as the main deity, in voodoo He has very little to do with the daily lives of the people of this world. Those duties are delegated to the spirits.

The main job of the average person who believes in voodoo is to appease the spirits through offerings, altars and worship so that they may remain in the spirits good graces. Doing so won't necessarily mean that they will have good things happen to them, but it will prevent the spirits from taking retribution on them in the form of evil occurrences.

Voodoo has been described as a folk religion (the name alone lessens the serious impact it has on the people), a philosophy of life and a health care delivery system. All are true to some degree as it applies to how voodoo is practiced in Haiti.

Voodun came to Haiti from Africa when the slaves were brought to Haiti by the Spanish. It has developed into its unique form of voodoo, but remains similar to its origins.

Haitian voodoo is a well organized religion which exhibits tremendous influence over the actions of the people of Haiti. It is practiced as a religion unto itself in the peristyles (places of worship) by the voodoo practitioners. Male voodoo practitioners are called Houngans (also witchdoctors-a more colloquial term) and female practitioners are known as mambos.

The actual worship ceremony is a complicated series of events. An intricate symbol which has been designated for the specific spirit that is requested to attend is drawn on the ground with corn meal. This symbol is known as a veve. Each spirit or spirit family have their own symbol. There are many because in Haiti there are many spirits and spirit families. The veve serves as a welcome for the spirit.

Dancing, chanting and drum beating all go on for various periods of time to draw the spirit to the place and welcome it. Various forms of animal sacrifice occur during voodoo ceremonies. All of this occurs with the intention of having the spirit that is being invoked actually visit the group in the form of a possession of one of the voodoo practitioners. The spirit will "mount" or "ride" the person being possessed.

There are training facilities to produce new Houngans and Mambo's. Many peristyles are seen through out the country. They are colorful buildings often with a voodoo symbol such as a snake, rooster or veve painted on them.

On a daily basis, the person practicing voodoo is expected to keep an altar which offers food, drink and other favorites of the spirit to appease them, preventing illnesses and untoward events. This occurs daily. Altars I have seen have been quite elaborate.

In addition, witchdoctors serve as practitioners of health care. Many people go to the local witchdoctor when they are ill for the purposes of achieving healing. These are easily identified by a flag which has a veve painted on it that is flying over the "office". You will see them often when driving through Haiti, especially in the rural areas. In the city, the witchdoctors will have their veve painted on the door of their establishment.

The witchdoctor will consult his/her divination book, a book with various potions and penitence's which are intended to help the "patient" return to the good graces of the spirit and thus heal them of their physical ailment. Prices are dependant on the particular spirit they wish to contact. There are illnesses which are viewed as natural illness-colds, cough, some infections. Others are clearly viewed as supernatural-caused by the spirits because of a lack of attention to the spirits needs or because a witchdoctor who practices black magic has put a curse on a person at the request of the unpleased spirits or an enemy. Conditions like strokes, seizures and mental illnesses are seen as supernatural illnesses. All of these will need to be treated by a practitioner of the spirit world and not traditional western medicine. Frequently in these situations, a patient will seek out the services of a witchdoctor before they go to a physician practicing western medicine.

Along with being practiced on its own, unfortunately voodoo has infiltrated the Catholic church in Haiti. Haiti is 90% Catholic. But many people will say Haiti is 90% Catholic and 100% voodoo. I have found this to be true within the non protestant community in Haiti. It clearly expresses the prevalence of the belief in the spirit world throughout Haiti.

When the Spanish originally conquered Haiti several hundred years ago, they allowed the former African slaves to continue to practice their native religion during their process of evangelization and conversion to Catholicism. They thought that if they allowed them to continue some of their own native practices while at the same time practicing Catholicism, it would make the transition and conversion easier.

It has had a very unfortunate effect on the practice of Catholicism in Haiti. Voodoo is intermingled with the practice of Catholicism to the point that in some places it is considered a part of the practice of being Catholic. Haitians participate in mass on Sunday and may visit the witchdoctor or participate in a peristyles spirit worship ceremony on another day of the week.

To make this point, I regularly take our teams to one church in Port au Prince to view a series of beautifully painted murals depicting various bible stories in a modern context. Very clearly on the murals are symbols of voodoo practice-an animal sacrifice, a cock and pig-both symbols of voodoo practice, drums, etc.

More importantly, the concept of the effects of spirits on the life of the average Haitian has infiltrated their culture severely. These kinds of belief are very difficult to change. I have often seen situations like a patient in our clinic who will blame their hydrocephalic child on the fact that they quarreled with their neighbor the week before the child was born, believing the neighbor sought out a witchdoctor to place a curse on the woman's child prior to birth. I once treated a witchdoctor in our clinic who indicated his stroke was caused by another competing witchdoctor. These are not uncommon occurrences in our clinics.

Voodoo is a religion and as such, practice of it will only further enslave the Haitian people, as animism in general serves to enslave. Along with the rigors of their daily life, the average Haitian now feels that they must earn the good graces of the spirit's by making further sacrifices and maintaining altars to appease them thus keeping them in the spirit's good graces. While it may not make their life better, it may keep it from getting worse-all of which only drains physical and financial resources that the Haitians don't have.

It is in this vein that I believe the tenets of Christianity may make inroads. Fortunately we cannot earn our way to the Father. The concept of grace in a culture where animism is practiced is a freeing one. Acknowledging and accepting that we are not worthy, our Heavenly Father has chosen to make the ultimate sacrifice for us and to allow us into His presence permanently without further sacrifice. We need only follow and obey Him.

Voodoo is often looked upon with curiosity by the people who become acquainted with Haiti. They find it titillating and may even desire to attend a voodoo ceremony. It is clear that voodoo and its practice and results are real. Given they do not come from the Heavenly Father, one can only surmise where the power of voodoo lies. It is with the enemy. There are dark spirits which are at work in this world and they are very alive in Haiti in the form of the practice and results of voodoo.

Voodoo is not a folk religion which is to be viewed as harmless and a means of hope for those who practice it. It is a chain of bondage which further entraps people whose lives are difficult. Only through the saving grace of God can these bonds be broken. Voodoo is real and a real force to be reckoned with in Haiti. There are many rumors and legends about the power of Satan on the island of Haiti. Many will tell you the island has been sold to the devil at various times in their history by their leaders. This deal was sealed through commitment to the practice of voodoo. These stories are powerful and have an impact on the average Haitian. In 2002, Aristide declared voodoo an official religion in Haiti acknowledging and giving credibility to its practice.

Christianity is the only way to freedom for the Haitians. There is a strong Christian influence at work in Haiti. The forces which trap people through the practice of voodoo are very strong in Haiti. The powers of evil are not happy with works like Pastor Auguste's or Pastor Charles.

If we are to be effective in spreading the gospel in Haiti, voodoo is a force and influence in the culture which we must acknowledge as a powerful influence on the Haitian people and one that must be taken very seriously. Strategies to emphasize the freeing grace of the God of the universe will need to be developed in order to break this powerful cultural influence in Haiti.

CHAPTER FOURTEEN

The Road to Garema

*"Enter through the narrow gate. For wide is the gate and broad is
the road that leads to destruction, and many enter through it.
But small is the gate and narrow the road that leads to life,
and only a few find it."*
Matthew 7:13-4 (NIV)

The reaction of most people when they first view the road to
Garema, a small valley in the mountains on the southern coast
of Haiti, is unbelief. One can discern it as a road, but just barely. It is
a narrow white, winding strip that extends deep into the valley, slith-
ering, as it tries to reach the valley floor. The road is constructed, but
just barely. It is composed of crushed rock for the most part. There
are 2 small areas that were paved at some time. These areas are only
about 10 feet long and now are cracked and broken.

Garema has a population of about 7000 people. They are all
farmers and farming families. These farms do not resemble what
Americans think of when we envision farms. The land in Garema
exists on the steep mountain slopes that the road follows. Most, if
not all, of the trees have been deforested and used for fuel. The
topsoil has eroded away, leaving poor quality dirt in which the
framers try to grow crops.

Nearly all of the homes in which the farming families live are
shacks. Most of the time, the homes only have 2 or 3 rooms. All the
rooms are multi-purpose, sleeping, eating and living. Many are
constructed out of wood with a metal or wooden roof. There is no

running water or electricity in the entire valley. The only exception is the guesthouse that has a generator that runs 3 hours a day from 4 to7 PM each night.

There are no plumbing facilities in any of the houses. Community outhouses or latrines are near some of the houses, but not all. There is a fresh mountain stream, which has been felt to be safe for use for drinking. The peasants use this as their only water source. (An interesting side note: despite the fact that it was viewed as being "safe", for safety purposes, the guesthouse staff continued to chlorinate the water for any outside guest staying in Garema).

Many of the peasants are malnourished and some near starvation. Nestled into a small mountain crevice near the guesthouse are 2 shanty's that serve as an orphanage which houses 35 children whose parents have either died or given them to the nuns to care for because they can no longer do so. Many were near death from starvation when they arrived. A number of them still exhibit the distended abdomen and reddened hair characteristic of this state.

I looked at this road with a great deal of fear and trepidation but it was the pride and joy of the small Haitian community of Garema. Several years ago, a group of peasant farmers organized themselves to try to make day to day life better for them. They knew the government would be of little or no help. If they were to ever rise above their current lives of minimal subsistence farming, it would be on their own accord.

An association of peasant farmers was formed. In the last 10 years, they have formed a small democracy within their valley. After electing a president and other officers, they formed goals for themselves and decided what the best way to reach them was. The first realization they had was that they could not continue to live completely isolated from the rest of the island. They had to find a means to connect both the outside world with them and provide them with a means to get to the cities near them.

Thus, the idea of the road to Garema was born. Prior to construction on the road, the peasants followed dirt mountain paths wide enough to only allow single file passage to reach the paved road at the top of the mountain. No vehicles could come into the valley. Any mission groups which visited the areas for clinics, building projects or any other reason had to not only hike in themselves, but they had to be prepared to carry in all supplies they required to complete their mission. Needless to say, this severely limited the assistance that teams could provide this small community with, as well as anything they could plan to do for themselves.

Once the road was built, the community immediately changed. Opportunities presented themselves that would never have been possible before. A school was formed to educate the 600-700 children of school age in the community. The school itself looked much more like a cattle barn than a school. It had a number of "classrooms" separated by wooden slates spaced about 3 inches apart. The noise from the adjacent classrooms resounds to all the other classes and for me, it was nearly deafening. To say concentrating in this kind of environment is difficult would be a gross understatement. But the children do learn, despite these unthinkable circumstances.

The community, with the help and support of outside groups, raised money to build a new school. The construction was completed in 2004. It was constructed of concrete blocks, all of which had to be transported down the road.

But other, more important, things occur at the school. The children each receive one hot meal daily. For many of them, it is the only meal they receive each day. The also get a vitamin and iron pill daily and de-wormed twice a year.

Intestinal parasites are a huge problem all over Haiti. Poor sanitation leads to the development of these worms and their sequelea. Even if nutrition is available, these creatures establish a relationship with their host and deplete them of much of the valuable nutrients from the small amount of food they may have available each day. One can easily see the value of a de-worming program for growing children especially. In addition, they come in contact with the nuns who run the school and guest house and spread the love of Jesus to them.

The school survives through a child sponsorship program in which individuals, families or groups sponsor the cost of sending a child to the school for one year. This is a common practice in Haiti and many other countries. Organizations or NGO's support the operating costs of the school through the sponsorship program and sponsors can come to know and understand the life of the child they are sponsoring better through various forms of communication from the organization. 30 full time teachers receive salaries and teach in the school.

The new school has an environment more conducive to learning. The teachers receive training in conceptual learning instead of the rote teaching, which occurs presently throughout most of Haiti. Children will receive 2 meals a day when funds allow and quarterly de-worming treatment when full funding is reached.

As we arrived at the top of the road, the driver of the truck carrying the 40 bags of supplies and personal belongings for our team became very reluctant to take the truck 1.5 miles, nearly straight down, to the guesthouse where we were to stay. The road descends at about a 45 degree angle. Walking down would be difficult, but certainly manageable. Driving down was another story. One could certainly understand his reluctance.

After a little coaxing and reassurance that others had taken even larger trucks down, our driver Gilbert, did maneuver the road safely with our supplies. From a personal point of view, riding gunshot with him down the road to the guesthouse was no picnic.

But that wasn't the only time there was a reluctant driver unwilling to traverse the road and unfortunately the circumstances around that event were not as pleasant. We arrived several years later with another driver. Improper maintenance coupled with the results of torrential rains during the rainy season had left the road in a state of disrepair.

As he surveyed the situation now, our driver was equally reluctant to traverse the road going down—more concerned about getting back up. He had been having problems with the transmission in his tap-tap. We had many bags of supplies. We just didn't know how we would get them down if we didn't drive. I must confess that underneath I dreaded the walk back up the mountain in the event we didn't drive down. Reluctantly our driver agreed to drive down.

Of course, going down was really not a problem. It was bumpy and steep but the truck had no problem making it.

After our visit, a couple of days later, we packed up and readied ourselves to head back up the mountain in the tap-tap. The initial part of the road from the mission guest house is rather level, with only a mild incline. However, when we got to the really steep part of the road, the truck clearly had trouble making it. Despite multiple gear shifts to give the truck more power, it kept sliding backwards down the road.

Our group was composed of me and another American. Traveling with us were two Haitians who assisted us with translation and our driver. When it became clear the truck would not traverse the mountain road without help, one of the Haitian men got out of the truck and placed a large boulder under the wheel to prevent it from sliding back even further while we tried to figure out what to do.

As the group surrounded the truck surveying the situation to try to figure out what we should do, I immediately was filled with regret and remorse. It was at my insistence that we brought the truck down in the first place. Now we were looking at a mile and half stretch of mountain road going nearly straight up and no way to get the truck up. I was deeply sorry for my selfishness which had gotten us in the place to begin with.

Over the years of working in Haiti, I have come to see just how resourceful the Haitians are. Given the fact that they have very little, they often "think out of the box" in a way that is difficult for me, simply because I am used to having access to so many resources they don't have.

In fact one of the things I stress to people going to Haiti is that the most important thing you need to have when working in Haiti is flexibility. One never knows what will come around the corner in the next minute. Given the lack of resources we are used to having to handle things, we need to be adaptable to the circumstances if we are to be effective. In fact when I want to stress this concept, I will refer to a situation as being very "Haitian" indicating that we did what was needed given the resources we had to achieve the end result.

For example, here, my first thought was we would need to get someone to tow the truck up the mountain. But of course, there are few trucks in Haiti. And those are located in the city. There were none in this remote area of the country. As has happened many other times in Haiti, I just couldn't see an answer to the problem because my solutions were so deeply entrenched in my having the resources around me that I was used to.

So after talking a few minutes, the Haitians developed a plan. The driver would inch the truck forward as much as he could with the help of the other four men pushing. At the point where the truck would begin to slide back, two of the men would throw the two rocks under the back wheels to hold the tap-tap in its new position. This process would be repeated until the truck was at the top.

When they told me what they would do, my immediate fatalistic response was "That is a plan? How can we [really YOU] possibly push this tap-tap up that mountain?"

It was exceedingly dangerous to push the truck the way they described. The men were right behind it and if it slipped, it could easily knock one of them down and possibly injure or worse, run over them. I just didn't think that was a solution. But as I calmed down and thought about it, it became clear to me that was the ONLY solution.

There was no other choice.

Choices in Haiti are often very limited. This was one of those times.

My friend and I insisted that we help. We just couldn't sit and watch these men do this work without helping. But they were adamant—they would not let us help. So my friend and I took our places on the side of the road to watch. It was painful not to be able to help to say the least-but not as painful as what I was about to watch.

The driver took his place and started the tap-tap. Four men carefully placed themselves behind the truck-two at each corner and two in the middle of the back of the truck. The two in the middle were in the greatest peril. If the truck slipped, the men on the corner could possibly scramble out of the way. But the men in the middle really had nowhere to go to avoid the truck if it began to slip backwards.

When the driver gave the signal, they all began to push in conjunction with him putting the truck in gear. The two men on the outside corners picked up the rocks as the truck moved away from them, continuing to push with their other hand. The truck moved forward about 10 feet and when it began slipping; the two men on the outside corners quickly shoved the rocks under the wheels to prevent it from rolling back.

They repeated this process, moving about 10 feet with each pushing effort. I just couldn't believe that they could push the truck this way for the remaining mile up the mountain. My friend and I sat helplessly by on the side of the road watching this process. We prayed for our friends, asking God to protect them from harm. It was very frightening to see them so close to the truck knowing it could go out of control at any moment.

The men were drenched in perspiration within minutes. They could only repeat the process about 5-6 times before needing to sit down to rest. My friend and I scrambled to give them anything we had in our possession to help. We gave them all our water and handed out all of the snacks we had brought with us. But they only lasted about half an hour into the effort.

About that time, we looked down the mountain and saw our dear friend Sister Constance walking up the road with a pitcher of water and several glasses. We also remembered that in the truck we had a whole batch of rice krispie treats that my friend's mother had made for us for the trip. We began passing them out to all the men. They had never seen or eaten anything like this before. It was all we had but we gave them to them. They truly enjoyed them.

Along the way up the mountain, periodically other Haitian men from the community would come out of the woods onto the road when they saw what was happening. They didn't say anything, but just hoisted their shoulders to the task and helped push. No one asked them—they saw the need and just did what was necessary.

I have seen this over and over again in Haiti. Living with so little and in such close proximity to each other, people respond differently in Haiti than they tend to here. They realize that there needs to be interdependence if they are to survive. They haven't developed the strong independent nature that we westerners have— the desire to do it ourselves. They realize that the only way things will get done is if they work together.

We watched as the truck literally inched its way up the road. The Haitian mountain folks are often healthier than their urban counterparts. More often, they have access to food through small gardens. Their physical work in preparing the land for planting and harvesting does build a more muscular frame than those who don't work the land. Consequently, while the process of pushing the truck up the mountain was painstakingly slow, it was progress.

It took nearly two hours to push the tap-tap up the mountain road to a place near the top where it could gain enough footing and the incline wasn't so steep that it could go forward on its own power. It was a painful and dangerous process that got it there.

During those two hours, many times I confessed my own selfishness that contributed to getting us in this predicament. I promised the Lord that if He would get that truck safely to the top, I wouldn't ever ask them to drive down again. I learned my lesson that day. Thinking of myself only had put others in harms way. I prayed I wouldn't have to learn that lesson again.

There are other lessons to learn from that road, though. It would seem that the road that initially looked so ominous from the top had become a lifeline for the industrious people of Garema. It has, quite literally, changed their lives. The serpentining, white streak that we viewed at the top of the mountain leading to the valley below, now took on an entirely new meaning. It is the result of resourceful people taking their destinies in their own hands and succeeding.

Each morning as I arose early, I watched the parade of people making their way up the mountain road for various reasons, some carrying produce on their heads, others leading animals. With the principles and basic tools of self reliance in place, the 8 years since the road was begun and ultimately finished have seen significant improvement in the lives of the people of Garema.

How many times has God put us at the top of roads in our lives leading into valleys that looked treacherous, dangerous and thus frightening in the navigating? The view from the top looks like it is something unobtainable. We find, though, that as we walk the road, traverse the nooks and crannies, we must rely on His mighty hand to steady us through the journey. When we get to the destination, we realize that road was a lifeline for us to the Father. It is He who meets us at the bottom.

It was on that dangerous road that He took us to the place where we could see Him better. At that point, we can become grateful for the destination and realized that we couldn't see it from the top of the road. All we could focus on was how difficult the road looked. Instead of seeing it as a road of intimidation, we now see it as a blessed path that brought us closer to the character of Christ.

Over and over I have found that service in difficult times is what brings us closer to knowing who the Christ is that we serve. He has told us that it is in sharing His suffering that we are perfected. Traversing roads like the road to Garema are part of that process.

I pray that the next time I see a road like the one in Garema in my own life journey, I will relish the chance to traverse it, focusing more on what will be at the end and the power outside of my own that will get me there, than what is between me and the goal-knowing that at the end I will be closer to knowing my Savior.

CHAPTER FIFTEEN

Refiners Fire

"I will refine them like silver and test them like gold.
They will call on my name, and I will answer them;
I will say, 'They are my people and they will say,
'The LORD is our God. "
Zachariah 13:19

God is using Haiti to change me. Over the last few years God has been refining me more into the person He has wanted me to be through our work in Haiti and the example of the strong faith of our brothers and sisters there.

I have been forced to ask the hard questions in my life. How am I feeding the hungry, clothing the naked and visiting those in prison? How are those aspects of the gospel played out in my own personal life? How does the way I spend my money show God and others what is important to me? What am I doing each day to proclaim the gospel as it is expressed in Matthew 25? What message does the way I live my life give about how I value the poor?

These are hard questions to ask and I thought the answers were not easy ones. I have come to find out over the last few years, the answers are a lot easier than I thought—easier than I want to admit to myself. To see them, I need to get past my own rationalization or justification of what my life is.

When one really looks at the situation, the answers are quite easy to find, but much more difficult to practice. The reason is because I find myself holding onto things which give me a false sense of security through material goods, status and success rather than the knowledge that I am held firmly by the hand of the One who holds the future.

Caring for the poor is a **mandate** in our Christian life, not an option.

To quote a recent missions team member who had just spent their first day at the Christ's Church of the City clinic, "If seeing this doesn't touch your heart, you need a new heart".

Each of us has a responsibility to be obedient to Christ's commands in Matthew 25 to help those who have not been as fortunate as us, those who need physical care, daily bread, shelter and clothing.

I have come to realize that wealth itself is a neutral commodity. Wealth is like a saw— I can use it to either build a thing of beauty or to cut off my hand. It is a tool—nothing more or less. Wealth is not necessarily something to be shunned, but this gift carries with it great responsibility. If God sees fit to place it in our hand, like the saw, it carries with it great potentials and great dangers. Only by committing its use to Him can He spare us from the dangers that it holds.

I live in a country of excesses. In a recent Water Poverty Index carried out by the WHO, the United States was found to be the country which wastes the most water of any country in the 147 surveyed. In the same index, Haiti was ranked the worst — 147 out of 147 countries evaluated—for water poverty.

I waste a precious resource when millions of people across the world die each year for lack of it. I'm under no delusion that if I didn't waste water it would somehow go to help those people. But using the resources God has given me in a prudent manner is one way of showing others and God that I consider what He has given me valuable and my desire to be a good steward of it.

But my excesses aren't only seen in what I choose to waste. I have often had the mentality that if 1 is good, then 2, 3, or 5 must be better. This applies to everything from shoes, clothes, lawnmowers-

I have 3 (WOW-that is painful to admit), and cars, even things like houses. I have taken stock of what excesses I really have in my life. I have looked, really looked, at what I consider important in my life and found I live in tremendous excess just in my own personal life.

Recently I had an interesting interaction with a colleague at work. Most all of my colleagues know I do work in Haiti. As we were trying to decide on where to take some co-workers for a going away celebration, someone suggested an expensive local restaurant. When another person in the conversation made a sarcastic comment about the price of the meals there, I commented, "Since I have been going to Haiti, I really have a hard time paying $40 or $50 for a meal now".

My friend's response was sobering for him and me.

He replied, "Yes, I guess I can see what you say. That amount probably would feed an entire family for a whole year".

And he was more right that he could have imagined. Over half of the people of Haiti live on less than $60 per year.

So what has God been doing as He has helped me re-evaluate my life in light of what I have seen and experienced in Haiti? We often used the metaphor of a refiner to describe what God is doing to us in our Christian journey.

That metaphor is a powerful one when applied to my life as it has been impacted by the work in Haiti. Silver in its crude state is beautiful. But a skilled silversmith knows that to fully refine silver it must be held in the middle of the fire where the flames were hottest in order to burn away all the impurities. It would seem that this would destroy the beauty. Actually, it comes out with a greater luster, and a beautiful shine that we know as sterling silver.

The silversmith knows that he must watch the silver carefully so that he can take it out when it is fully refined. He knows when it is ready because he can see his image clearly in it when the refining is complete. The silversmith would never be satisfied with the unrefined silver because he knows the potential that comes from the process of refining.

And so does God. What a beautiful analogy for us. He knows that it is only by placing us into the fire that we can be refined. He is looking for the mirror reflection of Himself in us as He refines us.

How is God refining me through working with the poor, specifically the people of Haiti? I will say first that God has not told me to "sell the farm" (literally for me since I live on a small farm in North Carolina), take a vow of poverty, move to Haiti to work-not for now anyway. But He has begun to show me ways that I need to change so I can act on the gospel mandate to care for the poor in a more effective way.

First of all, I have prayed that God would show me exactly how He would have me enact Matthew 25 in my personal life. I have sought His guidance and wisdom through prayers. I have also educated myself through reading and asking questions of my friends here and in Haiti about how caring for the poor would manifest itself in my life.

I looked at how I spent my money. The way I spend my money shows God, others and me what I value in life. I have evaluated where I spend my money and on what. While it might not make a difference to the big picture where I, personally, choose to shop and what I choose to buy, it gives me a concrete way to keep the needs of the poor in the forefront of my mind. It also has freed up some resources to use for others.

I have looked to see how I can begin to simplify my life so that my personal needs are as few as possible. By doing this, I have begun to free up time, money and energy that I previously used caring for myself and my excesses to care for others as He has commanded. This will be different for each person, but it is something that has really helped me evaluate what my lifestyle tells others about what I see as important.

Fasting has been a wonderful tool to do this. In fasting, we are acknowledging our complete dependence on God for everything we do. It brings us in touch with the need to completely rely on God for everything. As our stomach growls, it is God's call to pray—for ourselves, our country and its priorities and for the poor in the world. It also frees up time we would spend preparing and eating food to seek God in prayer.

I have felt called by God to dedicate a part of my life to raising people's awareness of what poverty looks like in this world by taking them to Haiti. This book is part of that effort. Viewing poverty like one sees in Haiti will demand a response. My goal in taking people to Haiti and talking to them about it is to provide an environment where the Holy Spirit can work in their lives to show them what He wants them to see. I have no other agenda. I want to be able to help put people in a place where they can seek God's guidance in their life with regards to this issue.

One very important way God has changed me with the work in Haiti is to help me develop a sense of gratitude-and it has been a profound one. In Haiti, I have lived where the bathroom is the corn-field, the shower is a 5 gallon bucket with a ladle, and the water to drink is the local stream where others bath and wash their clothes. I am grateful for what might seem to be insignificant things like a toilet and one that flushes, smooth roads, a bed to sleep in that is not bug infested, a car to drive to work. Because I have come to know these people I lived with as friends I have seen the strong faith they have because of the circumstances in which they live. And I am eternally grateful to them for their witness to me. My own faith pales in comparison.

God has used friends in my life here to encourage me to take stands that may not be popular or politically correct. I am grateful to a good friend for his challenge to me on this issue, which gave me the courage to put these things on paper for others to see. There are many more ways I am being refined. They are not all completely apparent to me just yet and space prevents me from sharing them here.

Finally, not everyone can or should go to Haiti or any other part of the world-but I would eagerly welcome anyone who wants to go. The poor are all around us-we just need to have eyes to see them. They are in the slum areas of your city, in the Alpha course at our local church, 2 blocks away in a poor neighborhood, in the local jail, the state foster care program and yes, even sitting right next to me at my home church.

This is an ongoing process. Lifestyle changes like this are not things that change overnight. Seeking God in this area of our life is the first step, though. And I am continually seeking Gods guidance on this issue and trying to be obedient.

It took me getting out of my own life that was sheltered in that false sense of security which comes with material possessions, a steady job, and sense of success gave me. I needed to risk entering into a life where poverty of material and/or physical needs or poverty of spirit exists. Once I did that, I allowed God to begin the refining process which will change me into the person He wants me to be, the person Christ intends, a reflection of His image.

"Oh God, my god, earnestly I seek you; my soul thirsts for you…
in a dry and weary land where there is no water. I have seen you in
the sanctuary and beheld your power and your glory".
Psalms 63:1-2 (NIV)

I searched for God in the country of Haiti, a dry and weary land where there is no water. And I have found Him in the sanctuaries of the churches in the urban slums and in the poor suburbs of Port au Prince; in the mountain villages and in the rural village across the river.

I have beheld His power and glory there in a way I have not experienced before. But I have only seen Him there because His refining fire has opened my eyes to see Him. I am forever grateful for the opportunity to serve Him in this way. My prayer is that my painful process of refining will help others to see the image of this glorious God we serve, in me.

CHAPTER SIXTEEN

God is not surprised

*"I am GOD. I will bring you out from under the cruel
hard labor of Egypt.
I will rescue you from slavery.
I will redeem you, intervening with great acts of judgment."
Exodus 6:6 (The Message)*

"**G**od is not surprised by this."...an innocent comment perhaps. But this comment changed my life profoundly when it was uttered recently in a cottage prayer meeting we were having during the height of the political unrest in Haiti. This is how.

Just a month or so before, I had to seen friend's daughter in our clinic. I knew that we could fix the problem she had. I even knew that if a complication arose from the procedure which would be ultimately used to correct the problem, we could fix that too. I had walked this road with many families.

I knew what lay ahead. I had confidence in our team to diagnosis and correct the problem. Although, it was a serious one, and while I was concerned, it didn't give me undue anxiety because we had faced this problem before—many times actually. Because of that, I had confidence that I knew what would happen.

She had the procedure and did well. One evening after the fact, my friends told me that they had been so worried about this problem. They had spent many hours in prayer for it. While they didn't convey that degree of anxiety and fear to me, I must admit I was somewhat surprised.

Yes, it was a serious problem, but it just didn't elicit that degree of anxiety in me. Even though was not my child it was happening to, I felt I knew them well enough to have a personal connection to the problem. Yet I had much more confidence in what I saw would be the outcome—mostly because I had dealt with this many times before

As I reflected on this, and when I heard someone in our prayer group that night say—"God, we know you are not surprised by this", I came to realize a little better how I think God feels.

The civil and political unrest in Haiti from November 2003-February, 2004 was escalating. It was clear that the people were becoming increasingly restless with the lack of change which had occurred during their elected president's administration.

In addition, former military leaders were clearly organizing in a way that was unprecedented. In early January, 2004 the rebel forces, now very organized and heavily armed, began their move on the capital city. They began in the northern part of the country where they were headquartered and marched into small cities, declaring themselves as the ruling authorities from this time forward.

All of the small towns either welcomed them or didn't resist. Gradually, they made their way to the largest city in the north, Cap Haitian. There was a small skirmish but overall not much of a fight was put up to stop them.

Early in his administration, former President Jean-Bertrand Aristide disbanded the dreaded Armed Forces of Haiti — the perpetrators of numerous coups, including one against him, and some of the worst human rights abuses in the hemisphere. At this point, outside of the police force, there was no way to put up resistance to the rebel forces now numbering in the thousands and led by a former army colonel.

In late January, they began their march south. At each small town they surrounded it and declared themselves to be the rule of law. We were following the internet news stories very carefully. Each day we saw them moving closer and closer to the capital city of Port au Prince. It was here that the real confrontation would occur-no one had any doubt of that. Each day brought them closer.

As I sat here and watched the threat to the safety of the people I had come to love, I felt sick to my stomach. The students in Port au Prince were demonstrating each day. Police attempts to quell them led to even more violent confrontations. One administrator at a university in Port au Prince had both his legs broken by the police in an attempt to intimidate the students.

One of the students that Luke's Mission supports was in a leadership position with the organized students who were protesting against the current government. He found himself needing to go underground for many months because his life was threatened. While another faction opposed the current government nonviolently, they had little power and their protests did little but bring violence on themselves.

In late February, the day came where the armed rebels had surrounded the city with their forces. They sent messages to the current administration that, unless Aristide resigned and left the country, they would soon march on the capital city at all costs.

I watched helplessly as the rebels surrounded the city. It was clear that a bloodbath would occur if they marched on Port au Prince. I feared for the lives of all those I had come to love and felt so helpless to do anything. As it was, we were supposed to be in Haiti that week but had cancelled our trip as the threat to the city became clear.

The US embassy was actively evacuating all of their personnel. All the mission boards and main line denominations were evacuating their career missionaries emergently. The Dominican Republic army was assisting the US army in using helicopters to evacuate people over the border until they could get a plane to the US. The two seats on the American Airline flight that we cancelled were ones that were used to get two young missionaries that we knew out on the last flight that they had before suspending service for the next three months due to the unrest.

I had just spent several weeks in escalating anxiety, dread and fear as we had watched the rebel insurgents take over major cities in Haiti with some violence and loss of life. Police stations were ransacked and burned along with those that were in them. Many Haitian police who tried to confront the rebels lost their lives. The rebels continued their march and ultimately, surrounded Port au Prince for the final conquest of the capital. I had not heard from my beloved friends for over three weeks—communication which had been quite regular-at least twice a week before that.

I had watched this small country that no one usually pays any attention to and most can't even locate on a world map, make the lead story on the evening news. I had read emails from friends who were being actively terrorized on a daily basis and were now in hiding for fear for their lives. I didn't really know what would happen when the rebels took the capital city. I had no way on contacting our friends to even let them know we were having concerts of prayer for them.

We didn't know what would happen. Aristide was given two days to decide whether to confront the rebels or leave the country. Talks were ongoing between the US secretary of state and Aristide. It was the night before the proposed march on the city that we had a prayer meeting at our home for the specific purpose of praying for the situation in Haiti.

It was on that night in February, 2004 at the prayer meeting, my friend prayed "Oh God we know you are not surprised by this".

His answer couldn't have been any clearer in His answer to me if He had been standing in the room next to me.

"I have this situation in control, April", I heard Him say. "This isn't the first revolution I have dealt with. I have dealt with many like this before. This isn't the only country I have had to redeem from rebel forces. I have been down this road many times — some of the roads, with your own country. I know what is going to happen here and I am not surprised by this. I can and will fix this. And even if things don't go smoothly, I can fix that too. I have a whole team there. They are working for me and I am directing things. You know your friends, Pastor Auguste and Jean—they are on my team, remember? Those are my children in Christ's Church of the City and Balais. I will watch over them and bring them out. Have the same confidence in me that you have in the ability I have given you to help people."

While I don't really purport to know the mind of God, I do know that if I can have confidence in my own God given abilities to deal with a medical crisis with a friend, how much more I should have confidence in the one who made us.

This isn't the first political unrest He has seen. He has redeemed situations far more complex that what is occurring in Haiti. Those are His children there. He has not forgotten or abandoned them. There may be difficulties left to go through—most assuredly there are. It likely will be more painful before it is over. But even if it doesn't go smoothly, God is still in control. He has walked this road from the beginning of time.

And because of that, we can rest in the knowledge that He will carry out His will for our world, the people of Haiti and for us.

~~~~~~~~~~~~~~~~

Post Script

Three months later, May, 2004

Jean Bertrande Aristide fled the country of Haiti the night before the rebel forces entered the capital city of Port au Prince. He went to several countries and now lives in exile in the Republic of South Africa.

The rebels entered the city welcomed by cheers and joy from most of the people. Initially there was much chaos. A very violent period followed as factions vied for control. This resulted in, among other things, the main prison being broken into and over 3000 hardened criminals being released onto the streets. Most remain free to date. Through this initial period of instability, an interim government was appointed until democratic elections could be arranged a year and half later. The rebels gave them control. Their main goal was the ouster of Aristide and they had accomplished that. The United Nations sent in a multinational peacekeeping force to assist the police in keeping order.

A humanitarian crisis occurred. Hospitals had no medicines; there was little food available and what was available was terribly expensive. Rice went from $6 per bag to $20. Gas tripled in price.

All governmental services-not the least of which was garbage collection- were at a standstill for many months while the interim government tried to establish itself. Additionally Haiti was hit full force with two major hurricanes, Ivan and Dennis. Nearly 2200 people were killed and the whole city of Gonaive was underwater for weeks following.

The Haitian police force was virtually wiped out during the rebel overthrow. It had been associated with the former administration and was seen as very corrupt and violent when he was in office. Many of them were killed and their bodies mutilated and left in the streets. Those who weren't harmed abandoned their posts and job for fear of retribution. The interim government efforts to re-establish the police force in conjunction with the UN forces were quite ineffective.

While the violence continued, for the most part, it remained within the confines of those who were involved in the situation-the rebels, the police, the gang, other criminal elements and some former governmental officials. Violent acts were confined to areas of the city where the gangs operated. One could easily identify areas of the city to avoid and others that would likely be safe. The average Haitian was left to go about his daily business for the most part unabated. That would soon change, however.

We heard from all our friends. They were safe. They took cover during the height of the instability. The students lost 4 months of their school year and had to go until almost the beginning of the next year to salvage it. But they did. Gratefully, all our students passed.

Our one student who was underground remained so for months afterward. When we saw him only shortly after he had felt free to come out in public, he had lost weight and it was clear the turmoil had taken a toll on him. He remained steadfast in his faith in God and his desire to work for political change in Haiti.

Although there were news reports that there is a degree of "normalcy" in Haiti, that term is definitely relative in this situation. Electricity remained still sporadic. Our friends reported having access to electricity only a few hours per day and that is not predictable. The cost of food doubled to quadrupled and there was little available to purchase.

While the international peacekeepers initially helped to keep the street violence at bay, and secured the ports where the food aid arrived to address the humanitarian situation, there remained heavily armed gangs on both sides of the political issue. Retaliation murders were occurring daily. It was months until hospitals began receiving needed medication re-supplies. Aid agencies secured areas where food could be distributed to the masses. The interim government was in place, but there were many concerns from the international community about how it planned to function.

The interim government placed a moratorium on any governmental spending until corruption charges can be addressed from the previous administration. The police force was operating at a minimal level in Port au Prince only. Political retaliation killings were common on both sides. The other major cities had no established government supported police force. No other governmental services were operational in the countryside at all.

However, God's work went on. The new church building at Christ's Church of the City in the slum area where we worked was inaugurated on Easter Sunday, 2004 with over 2000 in attendance. During the height of the humanitarian crisis, with financial help from many friends Pastor Auguste provided food for nearly 100 people per day at the church complex-some construction workers, most not. During a two week revival, Pastor Auguste saw many people come to accept the Lord for the first time.

It was far from well in Haiti in May of 2004 when we returned. We didn't see much of a difference overtly—just more trash in the streets for sure, UN troops with their bright blue helmets in the streets now, an occasional tank. But the signs of unrest were there.

Haiti was on the verge of a major political crisis. There was still no real rule of law in Haiti. Police remain impotent to control gangs whose power is clearly on the rise and who are becoming more heavily armed each day. Stability and security are the priority needs which will need to be addressed before any other issues can be addressed. We were to see it only get worse over the next year.

CHAPTER SEVENTEEN

The situation here...it is very terrible

"...and I sat there among them for seven days, overwhelmed."
Ezekiel 3:15

I had just experienced one of the deepest sadnesses I have ever felt...

For some time now I had been desirous of seeing what the Hopital Generale, the main hospital serving the poor in Port au Prince, was like. We often sent patients there for tests or care which we could not provide at the clinic at Pastor Auguste's church.

The coup d'etat had occurred only three months before, in February, 2004. The resulting political instability had created a humanitarian crisis. Food was in short supply and what was available was very expensive. Hospitals and clinics could not get supplies. Electricity was virtually non existent.

The Hopital Generale was the only place the poor could even hope to obtain health care. Even then, they need to come prepared to pay up front for all the supplies and medicine needed for their care before consideration would be given for providing care.

We arrived at the Hopital Generale in the mid afternoon. I had been in other Haitian hospitals several times before. However, it would have been difficult to prepare myself for what I had just seen.

After we had entered the first of several "wards"-individual buildings which held patient groups by the type of illness they had-I knew immediately this would be difficult. The ward was dark. There was no electricity at that point in the day. The room was encased with bare concrete walls and floors.

Around the outside of this bare room, were beds which lined the walls-about 40 of them-each containing a patient in a variety of states of illness-some obviously quite ill-all of them very thin and probably malnourished as well as ill. Most, if not all, were men-I don't clearly remember. Some had family members either sitting or lying on the floor next to them. There was no equipment in the room-just beds lining the walls. The room itself was filthy.

I walked through the room, not wanting to appear to gawk at them and made my way immediately to the exit door on the other side. Tears welled up in my eyes but after a few deep breaths, I felt I had braced myself for what lay ahead.

It only got worse. The emergency room was really beyond adequate description. Probably 40 patients lying on the floor or on makeshift beds, in a number of states of disrobe, some completely naked and uncovered, some with blood draining onto the floor near them from their wounds.

A small child was lying in a bed with two parents beside him showing us his x-ray of a fractured tibia-a greenstick fracture-a fracture in which one side of a bone is broken while the other is bent leaving the ends the fractured ends parallel to each other. One woman was severely burned over about one third of her body and was lying there completely naked, uncovered and unconscious.

Several looked either unconscious or in comas. Some looked like they were in the active state of dying. Two people in scrubs sat behind a desk located centrally in the room looking over some papers. There was no real evidence of nurses, doctors or anyone else actually caring for all of these people. The only sign of medical care was that some of the patients had a plastic IV bottle hanging from some sort of apparatus near their bed, cot or floor space.

In the orthopedic/trauma building it was much the same. We saw family members sleeping on the floors under the beds of their family members who were patients. The smell was almost overpowering even to someone like me who was used to the malodorous atmospheres of medical care facilities. The internal medicine and pediatric wards were no better. For good reason, we decided to by pass the building labeled "Dermatologie".

As we completed our walk through the internal medicine ward about 20 minutes after this whole experience started, I became aware of a young man lying in a bed staring at me through very empty eyes. It didn't take much to realize that he had died—how long ago, I don't really know. But his gaze was one through eyes that remained open permanently-the blank stare of someone no longer in this world.

I had seen all I needed to see. I told my friends I was going to wait for them in the tap-tap. As I made my way to the waiting vehicle, I became completely overcome with grief. When I reached the tap-tap, our driver Joseph, was sitting in the truck in the back.

Part of me wanted to scream out—"Please, just leave me alone".

I really didn't want any consoling, or attempts to try to make me feel better at that moment in time. So as I made my way to the truck I prayed that he would not attempt to do that. Before I could even fully seat myself on the hard seats of the tap-tap, I found my face in my hands weeping with deep sobs of grief. After a moment or two, as I sat there weeping for what I had just seen, I heard the soft voice of Joseph.

All he said was—"The situation here-it is very terrible".

It was all he said to me as I cried without stopping for what seemed to be hours- but was probably closer to 30 minutes-waiting for my friends. Grief poured out of me like rain from a cloud-bursting onto a hot summer's day. What Joseph said had summed it all up.

The situation here—it was very terrible. And now I knew just how terrible. I had read about the general hospital and the humanitarian crisis as a result of the recent political events. I had heard Haitians tell me they could not go there because it made grown men cry. But now I had seen it with my own eyes—and it was terrible.

I have seen much in Haiti that would shock most people—even seasoned clinicians like myself. I even have been shocked a few times in Haiti. Out of necessity, I have developed a thickened skin as I have realized the limitations that we have to help people there whose needs exceed what we can realistically provide in the current political atmosphere.

I have intellectualized it all—consoling myself that I am doing what I can and what I think God wants me to do. I have told myself I cannot change the world but I can change the world around me.

However, the degree of despair and dehumanization I had just witnessed and the thought that one of the people I knew in Haiti might find their way to one of those beds-they most assuredly would if they were to need medical care-the questions to God of just how much people should have to suffer in this world and mostly WHY—all of these thoughts consumed my mind as my tears poured into my hands I could no longer intellectualize the horror of what I had just experienced.

As I contrasted what I had just seen with the image in my minds eye of the pristine facilities and cutting edge technology that I walk into each day to perform my vocation in a medical care facility heavily regulated by governmental oversight and rules protecting the patients we give care to—many of which I complain about having to follow—it was almost too much to bear. I felt like my heart would literally break.

When my friends finally returned to the tap-tap, no one said anything. They left me in my grief-something I am grateful for-but they were also in their own personal states of shock, sadness, confusion and anger. A hand on my shoulder during the drive home, a tissue gently put into my hand—that was all they gave and all I needed and wanted. I cried for three days after that experience each time I even allowed it to enter my mind. It is hard for me to think about, even now.

Yet as I reflected on this experience, another component of it came into my consciousness. I realized that my own life reflects brokenness like what I saw with each of those patients in those beds or lying on the floor there. I don't like to see my life this way but all of us look like those patients in those wards in God's eyes.

We are all sick with the malady of sin sitting in a darkened ward named Misery. It looks worse in some than others, but it is there in all of us. We live in a world that reflects the gloom, despair and inadequacies that were seen in each corner of the Hopital Generale.

As I thought about the sheer desolation there and my own lack of ability to fix what was wrong with the people, the inadequate facilities, the lack of trained people to care for them and make them better—I imagined Jesus walking through our world and seeing it like that when He looks at us in our broken and debilitated world..

As He walks through the wards of this world, the wards labeled Strife, Hatred, Greed, Jealousy, Pride and sees us sitting in the darkened rooms there looking much like the patients I saw in Haiti —I know His heart is nearly broken with sadness and grief as mine was. And how much more it must be—given we are the creation He loves with all of His being.

I didn't even know a single person in that hospital and my grief was nearly overwhelming. How much more would the Christ who loves us as His own, see each of us as one of those people lying in various of states of brokenness, illness and despair, feel the pain of our suffering?

As He walks through the wards of this world, did he, like Joseph our driver, say—- "The situation here... it is very terrible".

It is clear to me that He did.

I can acknowledge this situation is terrible; I can do nothing to redeem it. I lack the resources- physical, financial, political and otherwise-to change anything that I saw there. My inadequacies stared me full in the face and were never any clearer to me than when I walked through that place. I was completely helpless to do anything. My skills, talents and knowledge could not change this horrible place.

But Christ did walk through the Hopital Generale of this world. He felt grief, pain, sorrow and was broken hearted over the sin we have mired ourselves in and said, "The situation here... it is very terrible. I can, I must and I will redeem these, my beloved children. I will give my life for them. Their healing will begin now."

And that is what He did say on that first Good Friday.

Christ has come into our world to heal us, to discharge us from the wards of sin that we find ourselves in each and every day. I am one of those people in the beds on the wards of sin. I am lying on the floor there with the blood from the wounds of sin pouring onto the floor around me. My pride and jealousy have caused sores on the surface of my heart and have even eroded deep, in some places. We all are emaciated, sick, bleeding, and have broken lives in His sight.

But His grief called Him to action-an action which cost the ultimate price— the price of His life. Christ paid the cost to heal us. It was a great cost and one without which we would never be healed. It is something for which I will be eternally grateful, literally.

> *"Lord, I was dead. I could not move my lifeless soul*
> *from sin's dark grave.*
> *But now the pow'r of life you gave has raised me*
> *up-to know your love"*[5]

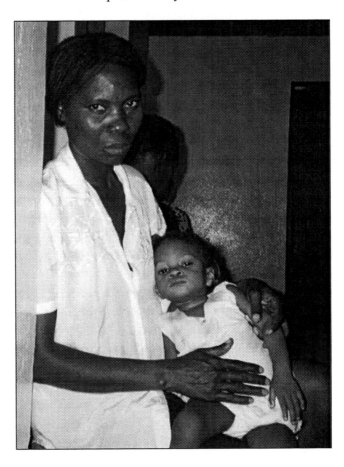

CHAPTER EIGHTEEN

Ransomed

"Oh come, oh come Emmanuel and ransom captive Israel"[7]
"This blood is for thy ransom paid, I died that thou mayst live"[8]
*"When from my dying bed my ransomed soul shall rise,
Jesus paid it all shall rend the vaulted skies"*[9]

These kinds of lyrics have been a part of my worship for as long as I can remember. I remember growing up singing one of my favorite songs, *Give of your best to the Master*-"He gave Himself for your ransom, gave up His glory above."[10] I could tell you what Christ gave so that I might be redeemed. But I admit those words rolled off my lips with really very little thought...that is until that fateful day in July, 2004.

I stood in church that momentous Sunday, only hours after a close friend and dear sister in the Lord from Haiti had been delivered from her captives by a ransom. We sang those lyrics that morning. Because of what I had been through in the last 48 hours, when it came to time to sing them, the words haunted me so much, they choked in my throat.

~~~~~~~

Two Days Earlier

I was sitting at my desk on an uneventful Friday morning when a pop up message came on my computer indicating that I had a new email message. I pulled it up and saw it was from a friend who also does medical mission work in Haiti. How good it would be to hear from her-or so I thought.

When I read the message, I felt sick to my stomach:

"I have just received word that Jean [Pastor Auguste's wife] has been kidnapped. She is being held by several armed men. I don't know anything else but will let you know when I hear anything"

I was in shock when I read this email but I stayed my response. From previous experience, I know how sometimes messages from Haiti can get distorted and changed as they pass from person to person. We try to keep all of our friends informed when we receive information from our contacts in Haiti. However, in attempting to do that, it is often misunderstood or distorted—much like the child's game of telephone. Add to that the variables of language, translation and culture and one can see how sometimes the message that I end up receiving is far from what the original information was.

I spent the next thirty minutes trying to contact my friend by phone. Before I passed this information along, I wanted to make sure it was accurate. When I got her, she did confirm that she had received a call from a Haitian pastor friend who knew for a fact that Jean had been kidnapped that morning.

That morning was no different than any other morning for Jean, our Haitian pastor's wife who served as the principal of the school at the Christ's Church of the City complex. The school year had ended and Jean was planning on tying up some of the details that day. She was up early-as all Haitians are. Because of the sporadic nature and/or availability of electricity, the Haitians work with the daylight. To be up at 5 AM was a routine thing for them. She was ready and on the road by 7 AM.

Although there had been unrest recently, she was astute in her decision making. She was very aware of her surroundings today as she was every day. Additionally, she knew many of the gang members and other criminals in the slum and they her. There had never been any kind of threat by them before. In fact some of their children went to her school.

She was driving in her four wheel drive vehicle to Christ's Church of the City complex where the church school is located. As she entered the road near the church complex, she noticed a man in the road ahead of her. That, in and of itself, was not unusual.

People walk everywhere in Haiti. They are quite skilled at dodging the traffic on a busy street. They are experts at it-even young children. There are few rules of the road in Haiti and certainly almost none that are really enforced. I grew up learning to drive in Boston, Massachusetts-known for the chaotic nature of the traffic there. But it is nothing compared to driving in Haiti. There are only one or two working traffic lights in the capital city of Port au Prince. So the saying "Possession in nine tenths of the law" really applies to the streets in Haiti.

However, as she approached this man, something seemed a little different. But by the time she realized it, it was too late. The man had a gun. He thrust it in the window and opened her door as he jumped in. As he shoved her over to the center of the car, two other men jumped in the other side from the side of the road where she hadn't seen them.

While the first man quickly took control of the car and sped away, the other men, just as quickly, blindfold Jean at gunpoint. She began screaming and yelling. The first words out of her mouth in this terrifying situation are chilling.

"This is the Lord's car. Get out of it. He will not let you have it.", she cried.

Amazing...that the first thing this woman of God would think of in a life threatening situation was the fact that the car she was driving belonged to the Lord and those who took it risked His wrath. Despite the tremendous peace that she said she felt, she still had the will and wherewithal that would ultimately help her communicate effectively with her captors.

She had been carrying her backpack that morning. She used this as a combination purse/briefcase. As it got in the way of the kidnappers, and they attempted to throw it out the window, she begged them not to. Inside the backpack, among other things was a Ziploc® bag containing personal hygiene items like soap and toothbrush and toothpaste. A church from North Carolina had sent many packets like this down to the school. They had just distributed them the day before and she had taken hers with her. She hadn't removed it the night before. Additionally there were the report cards she was going to be working on that day.

She asked them not to throw the backpack out. The report cards were critical to her work and the children at her school needed them. Could they please not discard them? For an unknown reason, they complied.

They took her to an unknown place, still blindfolded. She remained so throughout most of her captivity. As the day wore on, she began to talk to her abductors through her blindfold. She learned they had children too; that they had been asked to take her by someone higher up in the criminal food chain in order to secure money for their gang activities and that they would give her back when they received the $500,000 dollars they had asked for.

Meanwhile, back in the United States, when I did confirm that the facts were true, I emailed everyone I knew who was involved in Haiti work with the few facts that I knew and asked that they start praying. I decided to call one local friend who was at work in the medical center. I didn't want her to find out through an impersonal email.

When she picked up the phone I said, "Debbie, are you at a place where you can talk. This is serious."

I knew Debbie worked in health care like me and I wanted to make sure she was at a place where she could receive this news without compromise to her work.

"Yes", she answered.

"I just got an email saying that Jean has been kidnapped and I have confirmed that it is true."

There was nothing but silence on the other end of the phone.

When it lasted longer than I thought appropriate, I asked, "Are you alright?"

I knew she was and she was going through what I gone through when I had first read the email. But I had to ask. She said yes and couldn't really say anything else.

"Just pray and I will let you know if I hear anything." I answered as I hung the phone up.

As I sat at my desk with my head in my hands crying, I began earnestly asking God to keep Jean safe until this was worked out. It took all I could to compose myself and make some attempt to keep working through the rest of the day.

I was leaving that afternoon, with my good friend, to attend a wedding the next day in another state. Our flight left late in the afternoon. Before we left, I made sure all my friends who might get word on the situation, had my cell phone number so they could keep me apprised.

Although many people wanted to show their love and support in this situation, we had been advised not to call Pastor Auguste in Haiti as he needed to keep the phone lines open for the kidnappers. We were aware of the initial ransom demand and wondered how it could get paid. The non profit that supported his work did not have that kind of money available. In addition, some in the group had a moral objection to paying ransom in situations like this. All were encouraged to pray fervently.

Jean remained calm and had a peace which she described as one the Lord had given her heart. On Friday evening, when the time came to prepare for the night, the guard indicated that he would obtain the needed personal items for her to prepare for sleep. She told him that wasn't necessary.

"The Lord knew this would happen to me today, so He prepared me", she said.

"What are you talking about?" her captor replied.

"If you will just get me my backpack, you will see that I have everything I need", she said.

To his surprise, when he opened the backpack, he found the Ziploc® bag with the hygiene items that she had received from the church in the US. He was amazed. He began to believe that God really might be orchestrating things now and maybe they weren't completely in his control. No one carries those kinds of things with them to school. He began to have second thoughts.

She insisted that he leave her alone to prepare for the night. She was, after all, a proper Haitian woman, even in her captivity. She would not care for herself in front of a man other than her husband. She also requested that he remove her blindfold. When he did, she was able to see a few little things which gave her an indication of where she was being held.

On Saturday morning, Auguste was still frantically trying to figure out what to do. He had talked to the head of the captors many times. They knew he had friends in the US and demanded that the original demand of $500,000 be kept or she would be harmed. At one point, he told his church elders, who were maintaining vigil with him that he needed time just to be alone to pray. During this time he felt God strengthening him to do what would be needed.

He spoke again to the captors and told them that he couldn't raise $500,000 even from his friends in the US. He told them that the Americans didn't believe in paying ransom and would not agree to pay any amount of money-even though he knew this was not true. He indicated that he had about $5000 in his bank account and he would bring that and that was all. We were to find out later that the people in the area of the church-people so poor they cannot feed themselves or their children-had collected money that they had and offered it to him for payment for Jean's release.

After several more discussions by late Saturday afternoon, the kidnappers agreed to accept $5000.

At the same time, during the early evening on Saturday, Jean felt the peace of God in her situation. She had a chance to talk and pray with the man who was guarding her. When she prayed with her kidnapper, she asked God to provide a way out of the life he was leading. He told her that he did realize the error of his ways but felt that he was in too deep to do anything about it now.

"Please give me your address. I am going to try to stop doing the things I am doing and I want to write to you and tell you that I have kept my word", he said.

She felt that the Holy Spirit was clearly working in this man's life and wanted more than ever to be the vessel that He would use to touch her captor's life. At one point in the early evening, before he would do anything else, Auguste insisted that he be allowed to hear Jean's voice so that he would know she was truly alive. The kidnappers allowed this but only for a moment.

The leader of the gang who had perpetrated this event made a showing at the location where she was being held on Saturday evening. He told her that he realized then that they had made a mistake and kidnapped the wrong person. They didn't realize that Auguste was a pastor and knowing they had a pastor's wife only increased their apprehension. But, because of the chance that they would loose respect with other gang members, they had to go forward with the ransom. In retrospect, it is likely this had something to do with their agreement to take far less money.

Back in the United States, we were at our friends wedding but weren't feeling too festive. We tried to relish in the joy that would surround an occasion such as the wedding of two really wonderful young people. But I must admit my heart just wasn't there. We had been in touch by phone with Pastor Auguste earlier in the day for a brief time to share our love and support.

We didn't know any of the details of what was happening just that Auguste had asked for specific prayer as he continued to negotiate with the kidnappers. At about 10:00 PM we received a call on the cell phone.

"Auguste has left the house and didn't tell anyone where he was going anywhere. We believe he is going to meet the kidnappers. Please pray for him right now", my friends said frantically.

My heart was in my throat. What if he got hurt or killed trying to rescue his beloved? What if Jean got injured or killed before he could get her out? What if it was all a big trick? What if the kidnappers really didn't care about the money or worse—either of them?

We were to find out later what had happened. It was about 9:30 PM. His teenage daughter had gone to look for him in their house and was unable to find him. She had heard him talking on the phone to the captors about an hour before. Now he was no where to be found. She surmised he was going to meet them.

We left the area of the reception where we were. For the next 45 minutes we were in constant prayer-for Auguste to be safe, to know what he was doing, for Jean to hold on until he could get to her, that the kidnappers would see the error of their ways and let her go. The next hour was one of the worst I have ever spent. We were anticipating what the outcome of this situation would be— knowing he went alone and it was as likely as not that he would not come home either; knowing there was no real reason to set her free or allow him to leave after he paid the money.

Auguste went to the designated place to meet the captors. Money was exchanged and Jean was handed over to a very grateful and relieved husband.

About 10:30 PM we received another phone call.

"Auguste and Jean are both home safely", my friend said, the relief and joy apparent in her voice on the phone.

'I don't know any details but she is safe and unharmed as much as we can tell" she continued.

We praised God for his power in delivering her from her captors. An indescribable relief rushed over me. It was a relief like I have never felt before. It took some time to be able to really absorb what had just happened but I rejoined the wedding reception trying to be more involved.

I still didn't sleep well that night. That feeling of just dodging a bullet isn't one that goes away very quickly. In medical terms we would call it the fight or flight response-that surge of adrenalin which accompanies a stressful situation.

We were up early the next morning to catch a plane home. My mind was still racing, trying to make sense of what I had just experienced. One of the people I cared deeply for in my life had been kidnapped, held for ransom and released. Those kinds of things just don't happen in the happy farming community that I live in. Yes, she had really been kidnapped. It was surreal.

I arrived home early in the morning on Sunday and had decided I would try to get to church even if it was only for part of the service. I had phoned the pastor the evening before and let him know of Jean's release so that he could tell the people in church the next day. Many of them knew her from the work of our church in Haiti. They had received emails describing the situation and were praying for Jean and Auguste.

I arrived at church just as the sermon started. I entered quietly and sat in the back row. I just felt like I needed to be with my community of faith that morning. Things still seemed so unbelievable.

As the sermon ended, coincidentally-or maybe not -the song we sang was *How Deep the Father's Love*. These are the words that nearly choked in my throat:

> *"Why should I gain from His reward? I cannot give an answer.*
> *But this I know with all my heart: His wounds have paid*
> *my ransom."*[11]

I had just spent the weekend in dread, anxiety, fear and apprehension because I knew that my sister in the Lord Jean was even at that time being held against her will at gunpoint by captors who insisted that a ransom be paid for her to be set free. When I reflected on this situation later, I realized that many factors determined just what was paid for Jean's return. These were available cash, second guessing what the kidnappers really wanted, thoughts for how this might affect future events, and of course most importantly Auguste's great love for his soul mate.

When I sing about Christ paying the ransom for me now, it has a completely different meaning. Like so many things in Haiti, this experience has brought me face to face, in a way I had never experienced before, with the reality of what had to happen so that I could enjoy a relationship with the God of the universe.

I was more a captive than Jean—bound by Satan, held in his grip with more than guns-with the power of sin. I was blinded just as Jean was blindfolded, not aware of just how desperate my situation was because I couldn't fully see it.

As I think of the price that was paid for me, I am overwhelmed at what my ransom was-the life of our Savior. My heart is filled with gratitude beyond description when I realize that there were no negotiations involved in my ransom. He was willing to pay the price-the whole price without question.

It mattered not to him what Satan's motives were in my captivity. Christ wanted me back. Thank God He didn't offer partial payment or have to think about how He would redeem me and every other soul for eternity. Christ didn't negotiate for me. The call came that I was captive and He came down from glory to deliver me.

And in order to deliver me, He had to give His life. As He traveled that lonely road, in the same way Auguste did that night, there were only a few praying for his strength and courage. Most had deserted Him.

Unlike Auguste though, he knew what would happen. The ultimate price would be paid. And there was no uncertainty about it — *I would be delivered*,

But He wouldn't walk away with me. It would take three days before He would walk out. But walk out, He would and He would be alive.

Satan would not win, anymore than Jean's captors would win.

When I heard how joyful the celebration was for Jean's release, I was aware that I should be just as joyful each and every day that I, too have been delivered.

I have been delivered — not because I broke free myself, or because I tricked my captors.

My savior and Master left His life on the cross as my ransom.

Satan sat there and laughed gleefully, thinking he had won. But he was soon to see that his ploys are nothing compared to the omnipotence of the God of the angel armies as His prophesy was fulfilled:

"The Son of Man did not come to be served,
but to serve, and to give his life as a ransom for many."
Matthew 20:28(NIV)

CHAPTER NINETEEN

The Funeral

"If I live, it will be for Christ, and if I die, I will gain even more."
Philippians 1:21 (CEV)"

The next day was Sunday morning. Jean had been released around midnight, but she insisted that they go to the church. She and Auguste drove down to the church area at 5:30 AM for Sunday school which starts at 6 AM. However instead of going to Sunday school, they drove around the Christ's Church of the City area in their 4 wheel drive for nearly an hour, honking the horn, celebrating and showing the people there that Jean was free. They also requested that the people make no reprisals to the men who had abducted her. They asked that people show forgiveness and the love of Christ to them instead.

The dynamics in this urban slum are complex. Even those who didn't go to the church and whose beliefs were diametrically opposed to the ones preached at the Christian church, felt a sense of outrage that these criminals would be so bold as to abduct the wife of the local pastor.

There is a complicated "peaceful co-existence" that has developed over the years with mutual trust and consideration even in people whose life styles were at opposite ends of life's spectrum. So a call for peace and no revenge was needed.

Pastor Auguste and Jean didn't make it to the church for Sunday school but arrived for the Sunday morning service. When we talked to Auguste on Saturday he had told us that he was determined to go to church to preach regardless of whether this situation was resolved or not. He had prayed Saturday for God to give him a special message to the people.

Even during the time when he and Jean drove around the area he didn't have a clear word from the Lord just yet. He described it as "Pentecostal". Many people were thanking and praising God.

As the celebration continued, through the power of the Holy Spirit, Pastor Auguste knew what he should do. After the regular singing, he instructed the musicians to play three hymns that are traditionally used in Haiti as funeral hymns. No one really understood what he was doing. Their emotions had been so high and they were so happy at Jean's release. What could he possibly mean by singing these songs of mourning? They had cause to celebrate — not mourn.

After the songs, Pastor Auguste announced that they were going to have his funeral. Everyone was shocked and confused. What could he mean by this? They were joyful and celebrating. At this point, Pastor Auguste took Jean's hand. He and Jean stepped off of the platform and knelt on the floor in front of the communion table.

Auguste began, "We are having my funeral for my earthly life today. Today I am dying to the Lord. Our earthly lives are over. What goes on from this point is only Jesus. We are giving our lives in service and death if need be to the Lord. We will live and die in this area if that is what God wants for us."

Auguste continued as he quoted from Acts 20:24,"I count my life for nothing- if I can just complete the task the Lord has given me — the task of spreading the gospel of the grace of God. "

"I am dying to self at this very moment in time. My life is sold out to the Lord." he said. "For me to live is Christ, to die is gain".

From the floor as he kneeled, Auguste prayed, "My prayer is that my wife Jean and I desire nothing more in our lives except for the risen Christ. Nothing else! I desire for Him to completely take over every part of our very beings. We want to be completely consumed and taken over by Christ...even unto death."

This funeral proved to be a very powerful thing in the life of Christ's Church of the City. Many people were brought to the Lord that Sunday because of the willingness of one pastor and his wife to completely give their lives and death over to the Lordship of Christ.

For good and for bad, the story doesn't end there.

The one kidnapper's wife and children did come to church one or two Sunday's later as he indicated they would.

Eleven days after the kidnapping, there was a revenge killing of all the men involved. 14 people were massacred in the slum area in retaliation for Jean's kidnapping. All the kidnappers were killed in that gunfight.

No one was ever prosecuted for either the kidnapping or the retaliation killings.

~~~~~~~~~~~~~~~~~~~~

Postscript

While there is a clear testimony of God's faithfulness and witness as it is seen in the lives of both Jean and Pastor Auguste in this story, we must continue to see this event for what it was-a sin and a crime in which people were frightened and threatened against their will into doing what the criminals wanted.

In the process, $5000 of the Lord's money was stolen by them. As we seek for justice and forgiveness, I hope we can let Jean and Auguste's testimonies impact our lives so that we may become more "dead to ourselves and consumed with Christ".

CHAPTER TWENTY

A Heavy Yet Blessed Burden

"But the earlier governors-those preceding me-placed a heavy burden on my people," Nehemiah 5:15 (NIV)

God knows the Christians of Haiti to carry a heavy burden. You couldn't have gotten this far in this book and not sensed the heavy burden they carry. He has promised to be with them. But they remain financially and materially poor-not only destitute but lacking in nearly all material necessities, modern conveniences and resources.

They live in conditions where the heat is difficult-almost unbearable at times- in surroundings that breed disease, illness and sometimes death. They endure hunger, thirst, inadequate clothing, housing and medical care. In their futures, They don't often see where these conditions will likely change.

Yet, in these most terrible of circumstances, they have responded-much like Jesus as He shouldered His own cross through the streets of Jerusalem and endured the taunting and torture of the crowd. The Christians of Haiti have shouldered their burden with dignity and grace.

Just as our loving heavenly Father resurrected His son in triumph, the Father has responded to His children in Haiti. He has bestowed on them blessings beyond compare. They don't have physical riches, but they have wealth beyond measure. They have few, if any, material possessions. Yet they have an abundant store of treasures. They have little (and often no) food to eat. But He has lavished on them the bread of life. They lack clean water to drink and bathe in. But God has showered on them springs of living water.

These Haitian Christians have many blessings from God that we simply cannot access in the same way, not in spite of, but because of the burden that they carry for Him. I know this because I have seen, talked, and worked with these Haitians Christians. They will tell you in one sentence that they may eat one meal every other day-BUT GOD IS GOOD TO THEM.

Do we have any understanding of what it would take to say that and mean it? I have seen them make their way to the medical clinic through filth that most Americans cannot even begin to imagine. I know this because I have worshiped with them after walking the streets where they live. I have seen them get to church by way of the landfill that, literally, encompasses the street to the church. And when they arrive at their house of worship, I have seen an outpouring of praise and blessing to God, such as I have never encountered in our materially rich culture.

It was what my finite mind envisions heaven to be like, voices from all nations, praising God around His great white throne. I have seen faith in young Christians there that rivals the world renowned Christian leaders of the church today. They have no distractions to distance them from the Father, nothing blocking His abundant blessings. They must rely on Him for EVERYTHING-food, water, clothing and shelter to begin with. Consequently, they are like the newborn sparrows holding their heads up with mouths open to the Father to receiving His great riches. No difficulty with materialism, concerns about climbing the corporate ladder or managing a schedule that does not provide enough hours in the day to accomplish everything.

God has sustained them physically and blessed them enormously by increasing their faith in Him. At first, I looked with compassion upon these people and cringed at the burden God had asked them to bear for His sake. But now, I feel like the starving child, looking through a shop window of spiritual food, longing, desperately wanting those blessings in the same measure as God has given to the Haitian Christians.

I have been a Christian almost 25 years and my faith pales in comparison to these Haitian Christians. Had I paid my money for my first trip to Haiti and just been able to spend 30 minutes with my young Haitian translator, Remy, talking with him about his faith in the Lord Jesus, I would have considered my time and expenses a real bargain for me. My life has been changed by what these simple servants of God taught me in the time I spent with them.

The ultimate reward for these precious people will not be realized here on earth. But it is clearly promised to them in the words of Revelation chapter 7 (NIV):

> *"After this I looked and there before me was a great multitude that no one could count, from every nation, tribe, people and language standing before the throne and in front of the Lamb. They were wearing white robes and were holding palm branches in their hands... "Who are these", I asked the elder. "These are they who have come out of great tribulation. They have washed their robes and been made white in the blood of the Lamb. Therefore... He who sits on the throne will spread His tent over them. Never again will they hunger; never again will they thirst. The sun will not beat on them nor any scorching heat. For the Lamb at the center of the throne will be their shepherd. He will lead them to springs of living water. And God will wipe away every tear from their eyes" "*

Continue to pray for the people of Haiti. Consider becoming involved personally or with your family in the serving the poor in your community or somewhere in the world.

And ask God to bless you in the same measure as He has His precious children in Haiti-regardless of what it takes. You won't be sorry and you won't be the same.

CHAPTER TWENTY ONE

The Lone Starfish

*"But the needy will not always be forgotten,
nor will the hope of the afflicted ever perish"
Psalms 19:18 (NIV)*

During the height of the recent turmoil in Haiti, I received this email from a friend who was searching...searching for some reason for what he saw happening in Haiti.

~~~~~

"April,

A communication and a plea for inspiration. I was thinking of this story today. Perhaps you have heard it. I will share below:

An older gentlemen woke early, as he often did, just before sunrise to walk by the ocean's edge and greet the new day. As he moved through the mist along the shoreline, his eyes caught a motion off in the distance. When he drew closer, he saw a small boy, running back and forth along the beach, flailing his arms and dancing.

As he came even closer, he realized that the small boy was not dancing, but rather bending to sift through the debris left by the night's tide, stopping now and then to pick up a starfish and then standing, to heave it back into the sea.

He asked the boy the purpose of the effort.

"The tide washed the starfish onto the beach and they can't get back to the water by themselves!" the boy replied. "When the sun rises, they'll die, unless I can get them back to the sea."

When the older man surveyed the vast expanse of beach, stretching in both directions beyond his sight, he saw starfish littered along the shore in numbers beyond calculation.

The hopelessness of the small boy's plan seemed clear to him and he countered, "But there are more starfish on this beach than you can ever save before the sun is up. Surely you cannot expect to make a difference" , he said

The boy paused a moment to consider the older man's words, bent to pick up a starfish and threw it as far as he could out into the ocean.

Turning back to the older man the boy smiled briefly and said, "I made a difference to that one."

The older man left the small boy and went home, deep in thought of what he had said. Before long, he returned to the beach and spent the rest of the day helping the boy throw starfish in to the sea.

~~~~~~~~~~~~~~~~~~

Remember the inspiring story I wondered, what our response would be, if the story went on: "Looking back over his shoulder, the boy could see the very same starfish he was throwing, immediately washing back up on the beach? "

I confess to feeling that way about Haiti, and the efforts I read about. There seems to be no solution, not even an unrealistic one. We just bury the dead somewhere and build the huts back where the next rain will wash them away. I can't do it. I chicken out, if you like; I look for areas where my effort can make a difference, or at least have some hope of making a difference.

So, personally, do you see any such hope, or are you motivated by knowing a few individuals, and are inspired by the difference you can make in their individual lives? I just wondered.

Yours,
Will

~~~~~

I, too, had felt the way my friend did. His question is a good one.

What motivates me and the work that I do in Haiti is obedience—not results. The work that I have committed myself to is an act of obedience to the Lord who has clearly made His desires known to me in the things we are working on in Haiti.

A good example of this relates to a novel agricultural project that we are implementing in two places in Haiti. Aquaponics combines fish farming with vegetable production. The water from the fish tank is pumped through the vegetable beds, allowing the fish waste to fertilize the plants. The plants clean the water and return it to the tank so the fish have fresh water.

I am not completely convinced that our novel agricultural project will work in Haiti. It is clear it works here in the US and other developed countries, but I am not clear that is will work in Haiti. Initially, it has shown great promise and there are reasons to believe it will work there. But even if there were clear indications it wouldn't, I have a definite leading of the Lord that we should be doing this at this point in time—regardless of the results-or at least the ones I see. ("Though He slay me yet will I trust Him" Job 13:15 KJV).

Perhaps other things are going on beside whether the fish and plants are growing. Perhaps lives are being changed in other ways-my own included-because of the relationships that have been formed over this project. Perhaps this is the phase one and perhaps someone else will take it to the level where it will be successful in terms we can actually measure. I don't really know. But, like the starfish which the boy felt compelled to throw back in, I feel compelled by God to go forward, regardless of the "results" I see or don't see.

To answer my friend's question, in the example in the story, yes, I would be discouraged if I turned around and saw that the one I had just "saved" was now washed ashore again. However, if, when God said throw the star fish back instead of turning around, I kept my eyes on Him and followed him, I would be less likely to see the results.

When I saw the results (the starfish being washed back up again), I would be tempted to interpret this result with my humanness leading to discouragement. If I hadn't turned around, I would likely have continued to trust and obey Him. This would not allow Satan to tempt me to put my faith and trust in my own abilities to save all those starfish and not in God's to redeem the situation-i.e. use my humble efforts to save the starfish or other starfish regardless of what I saw.

In the example of Haiti-Yes I find myself very often trying to understand exactly what my feeble attempts will do in a country where the needs are so great that I realistically expect no make little difference or see any significant change in my lifetime. That thought is overwhelming, discouraging and defeatist. I could not go on if I dwelled on it in any measure. There are days that I do dwell on it and they are dark days for me.

However, when I keep my eyes focused on the Lord as He stands in front of me, I realize that He only asks that I follow Him not that I lead the way but only follow—what ever that entails. The following is obedience in all forms. When I keep my eyes on Him, I find that I can continue to work less discouraged. I am not keeping my eyes on results but on Him and Him only. It is really a freeing thought knowing that the results are not dependant on my "work". Obedience is all I am called to do.

That being said, I need to do all that I do as unto the Lord. I cannot take my decision to not focus on the results as freedom to not do things with all that I have and in the best way that I can. I must be diligent in service-giving everything, trying the best I can to make the results good, just not focusing on them as I serve.

"Junk for Jesus" is a common phrase used by missionaries. They use this to describe things that well intentioned people do or give thinking they are helpful when, the real situation is that, they are not helpful at all. My friend was the missionary administrator at a hospital in Haiti. She had a whole room she called "The Junk for Jesus Room". It was full of donations people had given, or worse sent down, that were totally useless to her. Had they asked before sending it, she would have graciously declined the donation.

Just because I am more concerned about being obedient than I am about the actual results, I can't allow my service to be 'Junk for Jesus". I must serve Him with my best. It is the only thing He deserves.

God will redeem the situation in Haiti, maybe in my life-time... probably not. It would be an act of God if it did happen. Certainly over time if He found faithful servants like Jean and Pastor Auguste, Pastor Charles and Remy in whom He could count on obedience from there on the ground, He could do it. He is, after all, God.

The main lesson God has taught me in this work in Haiti is to keep my eyes on Him. I suspect most Christians learn that lots earlier than I have. I admit to being a stubborn and slow learner.

What I have found is that my growth is not in the "doing" but in the "following" at all costs. I have found it a costly path to take-not financially but in costly other areas which are more painful than an empty pocketbook. My will is being broken, my pride toppled, my heart opened to the leading of the spirit in a way that I cannot adequately describe.

Additionally, I have learned many, many other things, not the least of which is gratitude—for my blessings-those I am aware of and those I overlook each moment of the day. I am learning humil-ity, what it means to really listen to others, to practice the power of presence even when I have no answers at all, and compassion-to suffer with others. But most of all I am learning what it means to REALLY obey.

My closeness to the Lord has deepened in the last five years more than all the 24 years of living for Christ put together that came before Haiti. I am grateful that God can and does use my feeble efforts to benefit others through His holy will. However, it is not me, but His power that has taken my two loaves and three fishes and multiplied them into things that have made a difference in people's lives.

My personal philosophy which I have felt the Lord lead me to has been that I have felt called to help "people (individual people) in Haiti" and not "the people of Haiti" (a country). God has showed me that my efforts are best used in making differences in individual peoples lives as opposed to trying to change a whole country or some other larger populous. That is not to say those efforts are without warrant. Just the opposite— if it is what He has called us to, we need to obey.

However, I must confess not knowing or understanding what God's plans for Haiti are. It will take God to straighten this situation out. Pastor Auguste himself has said that, if everything were to go right from this point on-something we really cannot count on given the situation and the politicians' there- it will be 50 years or more before Haiti can function effectively. If that is the case, it is most definitely something I will not personally see.

Finally, it is not just the field of missions that might lead one to the doubts my friend expressed. There are many fields of vocation where the progress is slow and not easily seen. Health care, cancer research, chronic mental illness, alternative power sources are just a few examples. Yet God is in those situations—ever redeeming them—through the faithful obedience of people that I look to and admire, folks who have persevered through dark times that seem endless-keeping their eyes on the light that the Savior exudes as they follow Him.

Keep your eyes on Jesus. Don't look back. Keep on throwing those star fish back in as He commands you. He can use the one or two that actually make it to carry forth His will. And if you hadn't thrown them back in, perhaps the person coming after you wouldn't have either.

When asked at one of the rare times she spoke to the press directly, how people could pray for her, Mother Teresa answered:

"You can pray that my work with the poor will not take my eyes off of Jesus"

May it be so in my life also.

~~~~~

"Dear Will:

Hope this helps.
Renmen, (Love in Haitian Kreyol)

April"

CHAPTER TWENTY TWO

My Life—
A "Designated Donation"?

*"He is no fool who gives what he cannot keep to gain
what he cannot lose."*
Jim Elliot
Martyred missionary to the Auca's

Many folks will find themselves thinking they are called by God to do something special at some point in their lives. But they will face obstacles. It isn't the right time. I need to finish my education. I am scheduled to get married. Let's wait until after the first baby comes along (Oh yeah—you'll really go then).

Having a call is not enough; it is really only just the beginning. What God needs to finish the task of the great commission-to bring the gospel to the entire world-are people who are committed to do that NO MATTER WHAT. It may require sacrifice in some form or another. At best it will definitely require inconvenience and perhaps, real difficulties at worst. But isn't it better to be uncomfortable in some manner and be in God's will than to feel safe and secure yet not be where His will is for you?

A missionary I know told me this story recently. She was home on furlough and went to get her haircut. The stylist asked her what she did—dangerous question. OK, did she go into the whole thing or just skirt the issue and say something general?

She decided to go for it and told her she was a missionary nurse in Africa. She described her work there in a remote mission Hospital. The stylist went on to ask her a few questions about what it was like to live there.

When the missionary nurse finished, the stylist was impressed— impressed enough to remark, "That is a really wonderful thing you are doing. But I could never do that. I just couldn't live without my Dr. Pepper."

I experienced a similar situation recently. A friend was introducing me to some of her friends and mentioned that I did mission work in Haiti. She asked me what it was like and I told her a bit about what Haiti was like-poverty, little electricity, latrines, no air conditioning.

"Oh, how wonderful that you would do that. I just could never go there though. I couldn't go anywhere that I couldn't fix my hair" she said.

How sad to think that something so transient as Dr. Pepper or access to a blow dryer would keep us from the will of God in our lives and worse, from accomplishing the purposes He has for each of us in His kingdom work. At the end of our lives, what if we looked back on what we did and saw that our "Dr. Pepper's" kept us from presenting the gospel to those who really needed to hear it?

Of course, it isn't Dr. Pepper or electricity for everyone. For some, it is concerns about health. For others, it is money, lack of what we perceive to be necessities-air conditioning, toilets, housing as we know it. And for others it is just a generalized fear of facing hard feelings and anxiety, worry that we somehow will not be able to cope or adjust to the external situations.

I have seen this in my own behavior as I prepare for a mission trip. Early on, I became an expert in cramming every single thing that I thought I needed into the one carry on bag that was designated for my personal belonging for the trip. As time went on and I traveled more and more to Haiti, my "needs" suddenly became less and less.

I realized that when I commit myself to do His work, God can give me the strength and courage to deal with a home made latrine. He could help me go for 2 weeks without any diet Pepsi. He could help me adjust to what it was like to live in 95 degree heat all day and night without any relief (I am someone who is quite intolerant to heat).

Now I try to take with me what is necessary but not really everything I need. And I suspect He will continue to whittle away at my perceived needs until I realize that all I really need is Him and commit myself to that.

David Livingston, the famous medical missionary to Africa's level of commitment is no less significant when he says:

> *"Lay any burden upon me; only sustain me. Send me anywhere; only go with me.*
>
> *Sever any tie, but that one which binds me to Thy service and to Thy heart."*

Likewise, the apostle Paul laid out to the Corinthians the degree of his commitment when he shared with them:

> *"Five times I have received at the hands of the Jews the forty lashes less one.*
>
> *Three times I have been beaten with rods; once I was stoned. Three times I have been shipwrecked; a night and a day I have been adrift at sea; on frequent journeys, in danger from rivers, danger from robbers, danger from my own people, danger from Gentiles, danger in the city, danger in the wilderness, danger at sea, danger from false brethren; in toil and hardship, through many a sleepless night, in hunger and thirst, often without food, in cold and exposure.*
>
> *And, apart from other things, there is the daily pressure upon me of my anxiety for all the churches." I Corinthians 11:24-7(NIV)*

It is this kind of commitment God is calling us to. Is going without our "Dr. Pepper's" even worth mentioning in the face of such commitment?

What we must realize is that God doesn't call us to anything beyond which He will equip us to handle. He wants us to commit ourselves, heart, body, mind and soul to Him. He wants us to trust with a certainty that He is going to give us what we need when we need it.

Corrie Ten Boom tells a sweet story of this kind of trust with her earthly Father. When they were getting ready to leave Germany to flee the country, she watched as her parents packed up their belongings and prepared to leave. She asked her father several times when she would get her train ticket to go on the journey.

After several times of trying to tell her "soon", he finally turned to her and said, "My child, you don't need your ticket now. I will keep it and give it to you when you need it."

It was then that she realized the love of her father, love that would keep her passage safe until such time as she would need it. Such is the same love of our Heavenly Father. He keeps our strength and courage until we need it. We need only to commit to follow Him, no matter what and trust Him for the rest.

The task ahead is a daunting one—that of carrying the gospel to the world around us, both near and far. This task isn't for the weak or for people who are unsure of their loyalties. The most difficult part of the task remains. And God will need only those who will commit to serve Him and follow Him through the rough times.

Thankfully, most of us won't be asked to sacrifice like Paul, who was willing to endure physical difficulties, or like David Livingston who was willing to be separated for long periods of time from those whom he loved. But He is asking for those who will be willing to evaluate just what it is that you "need" in your life.

He wants us to realize that all we really need is HIM. Like Corrie Ten Boom's father, he will keep our ticket until we need it. It won't do us any good here. We will need it when we face the trials and tests of our commitment.

Recently, I was asked by a friend about a supply I had requested that interested people donate to the trip.

When I gave her the answer to her question, I added "This is a very simple thing for people to get and it means the world to the people in Haiti who receive it"

Her reply to me was "Oh, of course, it is. And it is a lot easier for me to pick this up for you than to go myself."

I wondered what this woman was really referring to. Certainly buying supplies for the trip will make one feel a part of a mission effort. For those who cannot go, it is important to use the resources God has given them to help support this effort. But, it will also appease a conscience that is tugging at one to be more involved—possibly by traveling to Haiti. I don't know what she was referring to but the fact of the matter is that it IS easier to buy things than to make the commitment to go yourself. God is calling us to a level of commitment to Him regardless of how we assess our abilities or circumstances at any particular moment.

Shortly after we began work in Haiti, we organized into a small non profit to provide some structure to the long term work we were going to do. It was a relatively simple thing to do. I had the help of several wonderful friends who had various skills which were needed in the process. The main reasons we organized were to provide a structure which we could allow donors to contribute financially to our work and to provide administrative oversight for the work. We had several ongoing projects, including health care initiatives, scholarship funds for the health care providers in Haiti, and some miscellaneous projects dealing with agriculture and farming techniques.

Each of these projects had specific financial needs. We received grants for a couple of them. The grant is given in a single award, with the entire amount being awarded at one time. Since the scholarship funds are used each year by the students, they need to be raised each year from scratch.

In my role as Chairman of the Board of Directors of our non profit, I maintain the administrative functions. One of my other duties is to actively raise the needed support each year for our medical students. We give the money to the students on a June-June fiscal year. Unless we have raised more that needed the year before, in July our balance in that fund is near zero.

Our donors have the option of specifying where their donation will go with respect to one of our ongoing projects if they desire. Because of their particular interests in life, some donors are specifically interested in helping with the education of health care providers and prefer that their funds go towards this. Others desire to assist in the sanitation and hygiene needs of the Balais community. Anything that comes in undesignated goes into a general fund which is used to make up shortfalls in other projects or to cover unknown or emergent needs which arise or are made known to us as the year progresses.

Hang in there with me here. There is a reason for this lesson in the financial procedures of a small non profit. When I receive a check for the scholarship fund I am always a little relieved—knowing that we are one step closer to getting to our goal for our students funding for that year. I am also very happy when I receive a check that says "Use where needed most". Those funds provide us with the maximal flexibility in our work because we can use it where we happen to fall short that year or where we anticipate a need. If every check came in with that notation, we would be able to maximize the effectiveness of our work because we would be able to put the money into each of the projects as they needed them.

Our local church has a policy of not allowing designated donations. It is a good policy for this reason. We are a community of faith based on the teachings in the New Testament. As such, we need to work together for the common good. Any one individual's particular interest needs to take backseat to what is best for the whole church.

It is our elders feeling that if we allowed people to donate to their particular area of interest or for something that they want to see in the church, all of the needs wouldn't be met. For example, how many checks would read "Designated for toilet paper for the rest rooms" or "Please use this money to buy mops for the floors"? A missionary friend of mine calls these needs the "unsexy" needs.

When our church was recently approached by the organization that oversees Pastor Auguste's work to see if we could help with the health insurance costs of our Haitian pastor, this same former missionary gave our committee great insight into what it meant to "raise support". Someone asked her if she thought this money might be raised from some other source allowing our money to be used elsewhere.

"No, not likely", she said. "This is not a sexy need. This is the kind of thing that missionaries often ask their 'real' friends for"

I knew what she meant. It gives everyone great joy to sponsor a child and have some sort of tie to a real person in Haiti. It is wonderful to contribute to help build a church where you can see the beautiful new building or claim assistance for the benches or pulpit. It warms our heart to see a new clinic building or to say that we helped pay for the salary of a doctor or bought some piece of needed equipment.

But who sees the "results" of health insurance or the other infrastructure type things that is takes to proclaim the gospel to those who haven't heard? Who "buys the toilet paper" on the mission field? Who pays for the person to mop the floors or pick up the trash?

On the contrary, we are certainly aware of the need when it isn't met. Who is happy when they find no toilet paper in the rest room? Or when the lawn at the church goes unmowed? Or when there are no pencils to write with? Clearly, those needs aren't quite as likely to receive the "designated" donation but it is clear how important they are.

When I receive a donation that says "Use where needed most" I rejoice because I can see the big picture of our work. That is "what our donors pay me for". (I receive no financial compensation from our work, I use that phrase as an analogy only). I can see where we are going, what our projected needs are. We can see the whole expanse of what our work is. We see what the current work is and what we want to do in the future. We see how the projects are running and where we might have a short fall.

If people decide to trust us to use their money in the way it is needed most, the work will be more effective because of the flexibility it will provide us with. So those undesignated donations are truly the most valuable to us.

I thought one day that this might be how God feels sometimes. He sees the big picture and sees where His needs are. His plans are based on that. But we come along and say, "You can use me but only if I can work here", or "I am willing to go here but only after this event in my life." He can use us when we make those stipulations, but it isn't what His plan would have been. He can change it and make things good even with our restrictions. But how much more would the world evangelism be completed if we were all more willing to give our lives as undesignated donations? Would the whole world have heard the gospel preached to it by now and thus completed the great commission?

I am inspired by the commitment I see in career missionaries and full time Christian workers. They give up so much to make their lives an undesignated donation. It is not just full time Christian workers. It is stay at home mom's who give up or delay careers, students who sacrifice money, status to move forward in the career God has called them to, pastors, truck drivers, and many others-really anyone who had said yes to what God had called them to in their lives. It should happen in each vocation, in each life.

If God has called us, we should be willing to be undesignated by us and only designated by Him.

He sees the big picture. He knows the whole plan. He can see where the short falls are going to occur.

He knows where He needs you.

Gladys Aylward, career missionary to China for many years put it best when she described her feeling on why she was called to work in China when she said:

> *"I wasn't God's first choice for what I've done in China. I don't know who it was. It must have been a man – maybe a well educated man. I don't know what happened. Perhaps he died. Perhaps he wasn't willing, and God looked down and saw Gladys Aylward. And God said, "Well..... She's willing."*

As I pray for what God desires for me to do in my life to be made known to me, I want nothing else than to be, as Gladys Aylward said, *willing*-an undesignated donation for Him. I pray that He eases my fears and anxieties over callings I feel when I don't see the exact reasoning or when I am afraid or anxious. I pray that I will be willing to be used wherever the need is even if I can't see how my effort will make a difference, even if it is not in a place that is "sexy"—especially if I may never be noticed, paid a lot of attention to, thanked a lot or even recognized for my contributions.

I ask the Lord to make me willing to be the person who mops the floors or cleans the bathrooms or serves behind the scenes and to do it with a servant's heart.

I know those donations for the toilet paper and mops are just as important as the ones for the big new church-sometimes more important. I am grateful for the people whom I can call "friends"—those who are willing to make those contributions knowing just how important they are but also knowing they are not likely to get much attention—those silent saints. They are the backbone of our work.

Among the papers of a young African pastor who was martyred for the cause of Christ was found the following statement of commitment. It is a powerful thing to read and even more so to realize the faith and trust in Christ that this young pastor has to make such a statement:

I'm a part of the fellowship of the unashamed. The die has been cast. I have stepped over the line. The decision has been made. I'm a disciple of His and I won't look back, let up, slow down, back away, or be still.

My past is redeemed. My present makes sense. My future is secure. I'm done and finished with low living, sight walking, small planning, smooth knees, colorless dreams, tamed visions, mundane talking, cheap living, and dwarfed goals.

I no longer need preeminence, prosperity, position, promotions, plaudits, or popularity. I don't have to be right, or first, or top, or recognized, or praised, or rewarded. I live by faith, lean on His presence, walk by patience, lift by prayer, and labor by Holy Spirit power.

My face is set. My gait is fast. My goal is heaven. My road may be narrow, my way rough, my companions few, but my guide is reliable and my mission is clear.

I will not be bought, compromised, detoured, lured away, turned back, deluded or delayed.

I will not flinch in the face of sacrifice or hesitate in the presence of the adversary. I will not negotiate at the table of the enemy, ponder at the pool of popularity, or meander in the maze of mediocrity.

I won't give up, shut up, or let up until I have stayed up, stored up, prayed up, paid up, and preached up for the cause of Christ.

I am a disciple of Jesus. I must give until I drop, preach until all know, and work until He comes. And when He does come for His own, He'll have no problems recognizing me. My colors will be clear! Author Unknown

It is this kind of commitment that God is calling His kingdom people to.

The military has a group of men and women who are known as the Special Forces. Special Forces are highly trained men and women in the military service. Special Forces soldiers have earned the title of "Quiet Professional."

They are the most elite group in the military. Each member of the Special Forces must, by regulation, carry a medallion which is not to be any further away from them than one step and an arm's length. It shows to what they have committed. On the back of the medallion is their espirit d'corps. What is says is:

ANYTHING, ANYTIME, ANYWHERE

Are we ready to take on that motto as being part of God's Special Forces?

May our prayer be:

"Lord, may I be someone in your Special Forces that you can count on to do whatever is needed, whenever it is needed. May I be one of those saints who will be willing to get my reward, not here on earth, but in my eternal home when I stand in your presence. Make my life an undesignated donation. Use me for anything, anytime, anywhere"

The stories in the book show how I am trying to make my life offering to God one that is undesignated. It also shows how He is using it when I don't "designate" it. It is not something that has happened to me abruptly or at a single time; nor is it finished or even close to be being finished.

I have far to go. You have seen that in the stories in this book. I was afraid, made bad judgments, didn't pray when I should have and didn't put my trust in the Lord for the strength to do the work He had called me to as I should have. I will likely do all those things again. But I press on.

My hope is that as you read the story of my own progression toward being one of God's special forces, ready to do anything, anytime any where, you will be encouraged to push beyond what you see as your own strength and rely on the strength that God will give you as you need it, for what He has called you to in your journey with Him.

"This gospel of the kingdom shall be preached in the whole world
as a testimony to all the nations,
and then the end will come."
- Jesus-

CHAPTER TWENTY THREE

The New City of the Son

Isaiah 25

Our final evening in Haiti, a tradition among out team is to have a worship time followed by the Lord's Supper together. One year our pastor accompanied us and I asked him to lead our service for us. He shared with us several scriptures which he felt led us through the way of salvation as it might apply to the people of Haiti and thus to ourselves as well.

His final scripture, Isaiah 35, gave us hope for the future of our friends in Haiti. At the conclusion of the meditation, he challenged us to think about how this scripture as described in Isaiah might look when the day of the Lord comes to Christ's Church of the City.

I suspect he said that rhetorically, but I took him at his word. This is what I think it will look like for our brothers and sisters in Haiti when Christ's Church of the City in the City of the Sun becomes the City of the Son.

Isaiah 35

The dry and dusty streets of Haiti will be glad and the barren wilderness where animals graze in sparse pastures will shout for joy. The fields will grow many fertile plants. Like the beautiful hibiscus plants that litter the highways in Haiti, they will blossom abundantly. Many sounds of rejoicing and singing will replace the cries of sadness and sorrow now heard from the houses and places of worship.

The majesty of Carmel and Sharon will be given to it and beautiful hardwood and mahogany trees will adorn the landscape of the now bleak hillsides of Haiti. The faith that has been made strong by their difficulties will now allow the faithful Christians of Haiti to see the glory of the Lord with their own eyes. The majesty of our God will shine about them as bright as the sun which now beats mercilessly down without end on their land.

God will strengthen the backs and hands of those that have grown weak from many years of back breaking labor, labor that now only allows them to make $1.50 per day. Those who have lived and toiled in Haiti will hear the Lord our God say— "Be strong; your strength is in Me. No longer fear the bandits and gangs who terrorize you and your children each day in the streets where you live.

"Look now, for your God is coming with a vengeance; the rewards of God are now yours. He is here to save you."

Then those whose eyes have been blinded early from cataracts or diseases which are easily cured where care is available, those who cannot see because they have no glasses, they will have their eyes opened and see as crystal clear.

The lame man who can no longer walk because of painful bone diseases, the women who are stooped over from carrying heavy loads, those men who pull the heavy carts of concrete blocks or charcoal with their bodies like animals, these people will soon jump like an antelope and deer across the sides of the mountains.

Those, whose tongues have long been silent from disease or fear, will shout for joy. No longer will they be afraid to make noises and worship their God.

In the dry riverbeds where the only water available is full of waste, it will be here that streams will break forth and rivers will gush with crystal clear water. There will be no skin disease from bathing in filthy water; nor will any parasites be present in the water you find it necessary to drink. This water will be cleaned with the blood of Jesus Christ and will be flowing from the throne of God.

It will be the living water that will sustain you throughout eternity.

The burning sand will become like a flowing river and eroded mountains sides will become lush with tropical growth. The spiders, centipedes and mosquitoes that now plague you with many diseases will die off and no longer threaten you. Fields which are dead will be flowing with sheaths of tall grasses.

And a new and glorious highway will be where the Rue Nationale is now. This new highway will not be made of dirt and full of potholes as big as the trucks you now must ride in. It will be called the Holy Way-Sen Rue la.

Those who have not made themselves clean in the living water will not pass over it. Those who have threatened you and made your life difficult will not be able to travel on this grand highway.

Only those, like the faithful Christians in Haiti, whose faith has been strengthened by their trials and thus have been redeemed, will be allowed to walk on this way.

And those who have been ransomed by the Lord will return to this glorious new city, The Lord's City of the Son, Haiti.

They will come singing with joy in the new City of the Son. Joy will be with them forever and upon their heads where they now carry heavy loads on their bodies and in their hearts.

God will give them never ending joy, gladness and most of all peace. And all of their sorrow, crying, heartaches and pain will be gone forever and ever, for all eternity.

~~~~~~~~~~~~

Maranatha, please, O Lord Jesus come.

CHAPTER TWENTY FOUR

Haiti-August, 2005

But you, O God, do see trouble and grief; you consider it
to take it in hand.
..... you are the helper of the fatherless.
Call the wicked and evil man to account for his wickedness..."
Psalm 10:13, 14 (NIV)

~~~

"May your unfailing love rest upon us, O LORD,
even as we put our hope in you"
Psalm 33:22

~~~~~~~~

At the time of the publishing of this book, Haiti is bordering on anarchy. A coup d'etat occurred in February, 2004 in which rebel insurgents overtook the government of Jean Bertrand Aristide, a former priest who had become president of Haiti. A coup d'etat is nothing new for Haiti. Haiti has endured nearly 30 coups in the last 200 years. Each successive leader brings promises of a better tomor-row but none have improved the living situation of the average

Haitian and many have been found to be blatantly corrupt. All living former rulers in Haiti are now living in exile.

The summer of 2005 finds Haiti in a precarious situation. For the first time since the inception of the Christ's Church of the City 17 years ago, the gates to the compound were bolted and locked and the church stood empty on Sunday during worship time due to threats and violence. Gang members have made this area their headquarters. It is from here that they plan and execute their violent, terror activities. The school at Christ's Church of the city has been closed for the 2005-6 school year because of concern for the children's safety. The students have all been moved to another school in a suburb area due to the threat of violence. Hopefully most of them will be able to travel there and continue their education.

Insurgents are running uninhibited in the country terrorizing the populous. There is evidence that some of this is controlled via Aristide from his exile in The Republic of South Africa. Now, one year after the appointment of an interim government following the coup in February, 2004, 8000 multinational UN troops and police are on the ground. But they have had little impact on or shown to be effective in maintaining any sense of security. Instead, the situation has deteriorated significantly over the last year. Kidnappings have become the order of the day.

In the past year, all three of our ministry partners in Haiti were kidnapped themselves or had family members kidnapped. Two were beaten severely, leading one to spend time in the hospital. One missionary who was kidnapped has left Haiti. It is unclear what the future holds for that work. One of the Haitian church leaders was murdered for simply having a voter registration card in his bible which the gangs found when they accosted him. Our driver's sixteen year old son was murdered on the street walking home from school for no reason.

Initially, kidnappings were largely kidnappings for ransom - essentially a form of obtaining money during a time of low cash flow from drug dealings due to increased international security making the drug trade difficult. These "non traditional" business dealings were not netting them the money they needed. So abductions proved an easy way to gain income.

Recently, however, the kidnappings have turned from economic activities to political -an effort to intimidate and terrorize. As a result, the outcome of kidnappings is more often violent. Circumstances became more complex in June, 2005 when the UN forces, continuing their policy of targeting gang leadership, raided the urban slum where our work is and killed the remaining senior gang leader along with some of his subordinates. The effect of this has been to move the gangs further to extreme violence as they seek to destabilize Haiti through terror and ensure their own territories.

With no effective government in place, no trained or equipped police force, or other infrastructure for law keeping, particularly for the critical justice/security, health and public works areas, there is nothing to counter to the gang's lawless activities. The propagate evil unchecked.

One of the emerging problems is that the gangs seem to sense that mission efforts, both short term and long term, which bring light into life, are in opposition to the gangs' desire for control. It is all well beyond simple politics and is most severe in greater Port au Prince area, where traditional community is weakest. The police- who are poorly trained, poorly armed and few in number-seem powerless to maintain basic order. When they do, it is through a form of sanctioned vigil-antism.

Gangs have taken over whole sections of the capital city Port au Prince. Most of the major non profits and mainline denominations have evacuated their career staff and missionaries for fear of kidnapping or other forms of terror. Mission work, which literally sustains Haiti, is at an all time low. There are over 600 non govern-mental organizations (NGO's) working in this small island country. This alone shows the degree of need and effort that is being put into assisting Haiti with basic relief. The lack of short and long term relief and mission work which has been disrupted due to dangerous conditions, has led to a state of hopelessness never before seen in the lifetime of many Haitians.

Municipal elections, scheduled are scheduled for October, 2005 have been delayed with national elections being held in November, 2005. However, it is clear that there are forces working to produce the instability that will delay the elections even further. Kidnappings and general violence has increased at a dramatic rate. Over 150 kidnappings are occurring each month. Generalized violence goes on unquelled.

But God is working in Haiti. Despite the degree of terror, poverty, preventable illness, He is there. He is walking among the Haitians, down the streets of the urban slums; through the rural villages, up the mountain paths, seeking out tender hearts who desire to know His love-drawing them to Him through his faithful children there.

The stories that are in this book are real. They happened to me. And I hope you saw how my eyes were opened to the Lord Jesus Christ Himself as I made myself available to Him in service in Haiti.

If Haiti is to be saved, much like our own country or any other, it will be through the power of the cross of Jesus Christ.

May He convict us of our corporate sins against the poor and draw us closer to Him through repentance and service to others.

Pray for Haiti. Pray for Sudan. Pray for Iraq. Pray for the United States.

PRAY.

References:

[1]"Blest Are They" Words & music by David Haas; Copyright 1986 by G.I.A. Publications. All rights reserved. Used with permission

[2]"Follow Me", Words and music by Ira Stanphill, © 1953. All rights reserved

[3]"The Face of Christ" Words and music by Chris Rice, © 2000, Clumsy Fly Music. All rights reserved.

[4]"We have this Moment" Words and music by Bill and Gloria Gaither, © 1975 Wm. J. Gaither. All rights reserved.

[5] "Thread of Hope", Words and music by Marcia Henry. Copyright 1989 Manna White Music. All rights reserved

[6]"Lord I was Blind" Words by W. T. Matson; rev. *Hymns for Today's Church*
© 1982 Jubilate Hymns Ltd. admin. by Hope Publishing Company, Carol Stream, IL 60188. All rights reserved. Used with permission.

[7]"O Come, O Come, Emmanuel", Authorship Unknown, 8th Century Latin; Translated from Latin to English by John Mason Nealein, *Mediaeval Hymns and Sequences*, 1851,public domain.

[8]"In Evil Long I Took Delight" Words by John Newton, public domain.

[9]"Jesus Paid it all" Words by Elvina M. Hall, 1865, public domain.

[10]Give of Your Best to the Master", Words by Howard Grose, public domain.

[11]"How Deep the Father's Love", Words and Music by Stuart Townsend. Copyright , 2001 Kingsway's Thankyou Music. All rights reserved.

APPENDIX

LUKE'S MISSION, INC.
hppt://www.lukesmission.org

<u>Mission Statement</u>

L uke's Mission, Inc. is a Christian organization. We diligently and regularly seek guidance from God for the work we do to serve Him by serving the poor of Haiti. We entrust the work of this association to Him and will seek to follow the leading of the Holy Spirit in our work. We commit to not letting our work with the poor take our eyes off of Jesus and our daily, personal walk with Him.

We conduct ourselves in a manner which would be pleasing to our Lord and Savior Jesus Christ. Our conduct is governed by the guidelines expressed in the scriptures for Christians. All of our work is done as an offering of ourselves in service to God and the poor in Haiti. We welcome any person to join the efforts of this organization who will function under these guidelines regardless of religious affiliation.

Our purposes in Haiti are:
- First and foremost, to act out the mandate given to us by Christ to care for the poor.
- To foster the provision of health care in Haiti by supporting the training of Haitian health care professionals in Haiti and institutions that provide training to health care professionals.

- To promote illness prevention, treatment and public health education among the people of urban and rural communities in Haiti
- To assist in the provision of food, basic sanitation facilities and hygiene education among the Haitians that we affiliate with by supporting public health initiatives in these areas.
- To promote awareness of the needs of the country of Haiti to interested persons in the United States.

<u>About our name...</u>

Luke, author of at least two books of the Bible, was a most vigorous champion of the outsider. An outsider himself, the only Gentile in an all Jewish cast of New Testament writers, he shows how Jesus includes those who typically were treated as outsiders by the religious establishment of the day: women, common laborers (shepherds), the racially different (Samaritans), the poor. He will not countenance religion as a club. (Eugene Peterson-The Message)

Luke shows us clearly how God's love is for everyone. Jesus came in the world to be the Savior of all the people. In Luke's gospel alone are there several stories showing how Jesus used common or outcast people to bring God's love to the world-the good Samaritan, the lost sheep and the prodigal son. And only Luke tells how Jesus visited in the home of the hated tax collector and promised life in paradise to a dying criminal (The Promise).

An important part of Luke's story is the way in which he shows the concern of Jesus for the poor-the good news is preached to them, they receive God's blessing, they are invited to the great feast, the poor man Lazarus is taken to heaven by angels and Jesus commands his disciples to sell what they have and give the money to the poor.

As I have lived with and worked along side my brothers and sisters in Haiti over the last two years, I have felt much like Ezekiel when God sent him to the exiles in Tel Abib. It was there that he said "And I sat among them where they lived for seven days...over-whelmed" (Ezekiel 3:15). It was there he waited for the vision God would give him for the exiles. As I have dwelled among the Haitians for the last two years, having them minister to me, God has given me a vision for being a channel of His love to the poor by focusing on the basic human needs of food, water, sanitation and health care. Luke, known fondly as "the beloved physician" (Colossians 4:14), was also an evangelist. He served with Paul on his missionary journey and accompanied him during his martyrdom. It seemed that the mission God had given me and the work He chose to use Luke in were very similar.

Given our desire to show the gospel to the poor by helping the Haitian people have more and better access to health care while making God's love known to those who don't know Him, we felt that the mission of Luke-the beloved physician and evangelist-was the same as ours. Thus our name— Luke's Mission. Our prayer is that the Lord will be glorified through our work.

Organization Status

Luke's Mission, Inc. is a non profit organization. All contributions are tax deductible.

Statement of Faith

Luke's Mission, Inc bases its ministry on the follow statement of faith:

- We believe the Bible to be the inspired, the only infallible, authoritative Word of God. (II Timothy 3:15-17.)
- We believe that there is one God, eternally existent in three persons: Father, Son, and Holy Spirit. (Matthew 28:19; Ephesians 4:4-6).
- We believe that Christ is God. We believe in the virgin birth of Jesus Christ, that he lived a sinless life, and that his death redeems us through his shed blood.
- We believe in the resurrection of the Christ, in his ascension to the Father and in his final return to claim his children for eternity with him. (John 1:1-4; Matthew 1:23; Philippians 2:5-11; Hebrews 1:1-4 & 4:15; Acts 1:11 & 2:22-24; I Corinthians 15:3-4).
- We believe that, for the salvation of lost and sinful man, repentance of sin and faith in Jesus Christ results in a new life by the Holy Spirit and that Jesus Christ is the only way

of salvation. (Titus 3:4-7; Luke 24:46-47; Ephesians 2:8-9; John 14:6; Acts 4:12.

- We believe in the Holy Spirit whose indwelling enables the Christian to live a godly life. Galatians 5:16-18; Romans 8:9).
- We believe in the resurrection of both the saved and the lost; (Revelation 20:11-15; I Corinthians 15:51-57).
- We believe in the spiritual unity of believers in our Lord Jesus Christ and that all true believers are members of His body, the Church. (Ephesians 1:22-23; I Corinthians 12:12, 27).
- We believe that the ministry of evangelism is a responsibility of both the church and each Christian. (Romans 10:9-15; Acts 1:8; Matthew 28:18-20; I Peter 3:15).
- Luke's Mission's Statement of Faith, founded upon Holy Scripture, finds support in two historic source documents of the Christian faith-the Apostles' Creed and the Lausanne Covenant.

Haiti-General Information

Haiti is a small island off the coast of Cuba about the size of Maryland. It has a population of 8 million. The majority of these people live in or around the capital city, Port au Prince.

General statistics:

- Unemployment: > 80%
- Haitian children of school age: 3,100,000
- Haitian children who attend school: 850,000 (approximately 40%)
- Agriculture: Primarily subsistence plots, increasingly track gardens. Commercial crops are coffee, sugarcane, sisal, and fruit. Food crops include beans, rice, corn, sorghum, and tubers.
- Average size of family farm: 2 acres
- Cooking fuel: 90% wood
- Land forested: 6%
- Government-democratic first free elections early 90's.

- Average income $370 per year. 50% of the population makes < $60 per year.
- Population density: 670 per square mile overall, vs. 3035 per square mile in arable areas (compare with 22 per square mile in the US)
- Land arable: 20% remains productive; more is cultivated
- Potable water: 41% of the population has access to safe drinking water
- Malnutrition: 75%
- Doctors: 650 in the entire country (1:12,000 vs.1: 650 in the US)
- Infant Mortality rate: 0-12 months 17%, 1-5 years 13.3%; 30% total for the children under 5 years Infants born each year: 230.000
- Religions: Nominal Christians/Catholics 98%, Baptists 20%, Other Protestants 10%, Voodooists 65% (some overlap)
- Languages: French and Creole are both official. Creole predominates in society and French in business. English
- Average life expectancy: 45 years
- Illiteracy: -population-75% Adult literacy-48% of adults over 18 can read. The bulk of these people are from 18-30 years of age.

GOVERNMENT

The country has had a tumultuous history. Originally, settled by the Spanish and the French in the 17th centuries, the import of hundreds of thousands of slaves from Africa is what originally made it a very prosperous island for the elite. However, in the late 19th century, the slaves revolted, overthrowing the white ruling class and formed their own government, making them the first black republic in history.

Since that time, Haiti has had a number of ruling bodies, none of which have contributed to a stable political climate. Most recently in the 20th century, the dictatorship of "Papa Doc Duvalier" and his son "Baby Doc Duvalier" led to political instability for the country and strained international relationships. Widespread governmental corruption led to the misuse of international funds intended for social programs. Baby Doc was forced to leave the country in 1986 and Haiti subsequently installed President Jean Bertrand Aristide as a result of the first democratic election in Haiti's history. Aristide was ousted by rebels in a coup d'etat in 2004. An interim government was appointed. Elections are slated for late in 2005.

DEFORESTATION

The majority of Haiti is rural. Originally a country of lush tropical mountains, widespread deforestation has led to an erosion of the topsoil throughout the entire country. Where prosperous rural farms once existed, the land is now devoid of adequate soil to support crops and animals. Access to adequate quantities of food is now a serious health problem for the average Haitian even where farms do exist. In the mountain areas, families often have small farms consisting of a few acres. There, they may grow maize or corn, a version of squash or occasionally beans.

Some have a cow or goat that may provide milk occasionally. However, the fate of the animals in Haiti parallels that of the people. Many are severely malnourished, which affects the ability to produce milk or to be used as a food source themselves. Animals succumb to disease and illness due to lack of proper care such as vaccinations

~~~~~~~~~~~~~

COMPARATIVE STATISTICS
HAITI AND OTHER COUNTRIES

	United States	Haiti	Brazil	India
Population	282,000,000	8,140,000	170,400,000	100,890,000,000
No. children/woman in lifetime	1.93	3.98	2.15	2.98
Life expectancy at birth	77 years	53 years	67 years	63 years
Per capita income	$31,910	$460	$4,350	$440
Health Care spending per capita	$4,055	$16	$320	$440
Illiteracy men	1%	49%	15%	53%
Illiteracy women	1%	53%	15%	53%
Maternal mortality (%/100 births	1.20%	11%	2.60%	4.40%
Child mortality below 5 (5/100 children	0.80%	30%	4%	9%